LEFT
TO
THEIR
OWN
DEVICES?

LEFT
TO
THEIR
OWN
DEVICES?

Confident parenting in a
world of screens

Katharine Hill

Muddy
Pearl

First published in 2017 by
Muddy Pearl, Edinburgh, Scotland.

Reprinted 2017.

www.muddypearl.com
books@muddypearl.com

British Library Cataloguing in Publication Data.
A catalogue record for this book is available from the British Library

ISBN 978-1-910012-43-7

Typeset and designed by Revo Creative. *www.revocreative.co.uk*
Printed and bound in Great Britain by Bell & Bain Ltd, Glasgow

Muddy Pearl is not responsible for the accuracy of URLs or internet websites
referred to in this book. It does not guarantee that content on such websites is,
or will remain, accurate or appropriate. Sites were accessed and checked in April
2017, but may change over time.

Image copyright shutterstock: grynold and majivecka.

To our dear friends Silas and Annie, with thanks for your love and wisdom through the joys and challenges, digital and otherwise, over 28 years of parenting ... and still going!

ACKNOWLEDGEMENTS

This book could not have been written without the help and support of so many people. Firstly, a huge thank you to Rob Parsons for his wise input and encouragement. Thank you to the amazing team at Care for the Family, especially to Paula Pridham and Hugh Griffiths for commenting on the manuscript, and Rachel Harries, my fabulous PA. And much appreciation to Samantha Callan for her support and wisdom, and to David and Sarah Abell for their helpful comments.

Thanks to team Hill: Richard, George and Ellie, Charlotte and Will Caldwell, Ed and Catriona, and Henry, for fun, laughter and providing the raw material for many of the stories and examples.

I am grateful to Stephanie and Richard Heald and the team at Muddy Pearl – it's great working with you – and to David McNeill for the wonderful cartoons.

And the biggest thanks of all to Sheron Rice, our senior editor at Care for the Family, who has worked tirelessly and added incredible value to the book.

CONTENTS

FOREWORD

Somewhat to my surprise, I find that I am the grandfather of five children! Surely that can't be possible? Wasn't it only yesterday that I took Katie (my daughter) to her ballet lesson? And I'm certain it can't have been more than a few Christmases ago that I saw Lloyd (my son) put on a sterling performance as the inn-keeper in the school nativity play? But, no! The reality is that it was over 30 years ago, and in that time, a revolution has happened: a digital revolution.

Since time began, the role of parents has been to prepare our children to live independent lives. We attend to their physical needs for food, sleep, and clothing; we give them boundaries to keep them safe; and we seek to instil in them values that will guide them in the choices they will have to make, both big and small, throughout their lives. But parents today also have another task in addition to those I had 30 years ago. As far as I was concerned, issues to do with screen-time were confined to whether or not *Doctor Who* was too scary for a 5-year-old who was absolutely desperate to see it! But the world of screens that we live in today presents us with far greater challenges. As parents, we must help our children make full use of all the advantages of digital technology, as well as safeguarding them from the potential dangers.

In this book, Katharine Hill has tackled all the important issues head on and has given parents a brilliant tool that is full of practical wisdom and advice. Read it now ... and, above all, don't leave *your* children to their own devices.

Rob Parsons, OBE
Founder and Chairman, Care for the Family

PROLOGUE

The rain is hammering against Alice's bedroom window as she throws her school bag onto her bed. She can hear her little brothers squabbling downstairs. It's 7.15 p.m. and already dark, so she draws the curtains. She has a school science project to complete and turns on her laptop. Before getting going, she notices that Karl is online. He is 15. Karl speaks first:

```
Hi Alice. I've seen you on the bus. You're
in the year below me, aren't you?
Yes.
You're very pretty.
Thank you.
Alice, undo the top three buttons on your
shirt. [Long pause]
Like this?
No. A bit more …
```

And so it begins.

Before we dismiss this exchange as far removed from the reality of our family's everyday experience of digital technology, we may be wise just to pause and do a reality check. If current statistics are to be believed, online conversations of this nature will be taking place right now in teenagers' bedrooms across the country.

And many parents are concerned not just about the online dangers of sexting and pornography, but also the possibilities of bullying, addiction, gaming, gambling, grooming, and simply the increasing number of hours children and young people are spending glued to a screen. In fact, when we meet parents at our Care for the Family events, questions surrounding how to help their children navigate the world of technology leave all other topics in the shade. Many parents feel anxious and bemused. Not only do they have no idea what to do, but they don't know where to go to find the answers. A mum responding to a recent Care for the Family survey said, 'It's a minefield. I wish we'd never invented smartphones. It's just made parenting so much harder. Help!'

When my children were growing up, I was often so terrified they might make bad choices that it felt easier and safer to try to eliminate as many options as possible: no Wi-Fi, no screens, no going to that friend's house, no going to that party. But the truth is that although it's essential to put appropriate boundaries in place (and sometimes that means saying 'no'), just taking the default position of limiting their options only makes their world a smaller place.

Parenting isn't really about raising children or even teens – it's about raising *adults*. From their earliest days, we are preparing them for independence: the 2-hour session at playschool; their first sleepover; the half-term stay with their cousins; the geography field trip; the language exchange visit to France; the Saturday job; university. Each step leads up to the day when we will no longer be at their side: the day they leave our home and our protection. And for that reason, we must take every opportunity we can to build strong foundations – to sow into their lives the values that will equip them to choose wisely when they face different choices in life – and, in this context, the choices that the digital world has to offer. It's a sobering thought, but unless we do that, *our child will only be as safe as the least protected child they know.*

This book is written in response to the plaintive cry of 'Help!' from the mum who took part in our survey and the thousands of parents who feel exactly the same: *help is at hand.* Whether you are new parents with little ones or riding the rollercoaster of the teenage years, it is for mums and dads who not only want to 'cope' with bringing up children in the world of digital technology, but to be on the front foot.

Left to their own devices? – Confident parenting in a world of screens will not only give you an overview of parenting in the digital age, but most of all help you take the initiative and give you *confidence* in it. With strategies and tips that will equip you to protect your children from the dangers, you'll also be able to help them to

'Try to ignore the drone. It's just my dad.
He's a bit overprotective.'

embrace the wonderful opportunities that are there for them as they grow up in an online world.

So don't leave your children to their own devices, put your phone on silent, grab a coffee and read on!

CHAPTER 1

LIVING IN A DIGITAL WORLD

My alarm went off this morning at 6.30 a.m. as usual, heralding a new day. I groped bleary-eyed in the darkness and fumbled for the phone so I could swipe the screen and silence the sound. The slumber function would give me a welcome 10 more minutes in bed before the day began.

As well as waking me in the morning, my smartphone will be my trusted companion throughout the day. Dressed for this season in chic dove pink, she will tell me whether I have a busy day today – in particular, what appointments I have, along with when, where and even how to get there. She will help me decide whether to take a raincoat or sunglasses and whether we need a plan B for tomorrow night's barbecue. I can enjoy photos of our holiday, check my bank balance, make a to-do list, listen to music and podcasts, and keep up to date on current affairs. In the unlikely event that my children have consented to a reciprocal arrangement, I can track their whereabouts at any time of the day or night on my Finders app. I can remind myself of my favourite chicken recipe and even buy the ingredients. I can communicate with friends down the road or on the other side of the world, check out posts on Facebook or Twitter, plan a gym regime and, with my Amazon app, simply tap the screen to buy garden chairs, Christmas tree lights and dog food. She can even help me phone a friend! My phone sees me through the day, and the very last thing I do at night is to plug her in by my bed and reset the alarm to 6.30 a.m., ready to begin all over again.

Since I bought my own smartphone less than 5 years ago, she has revolutionised my life. My iPhone is my constant friend – so much a part of my life I am not sure that I could imagine life without her.

At a recent job interview, my son was asked which of the following people had made the biggest impact on world history: Mother Teresa, Adolf Hitler, Billy Graham, or Tim Berners-Lee. Not many of the candidates had heard of Mr Berners-Lee, but it was no mistake that he was on the shortlist. Tim Berners-Lee is a computer scientist and inventor of the World Wide Web. I doubt that even he could have imagined how his invention would bring about such a revolutionary global change. It has impacted how we communicate in every area of society: deliberations between governments, business deals between companies and corporations, campaigns for causes brought to the world's attention, personal messages among family and friends ... the list goes on.

History tells us that each generation greets every new technological advance with caution, and it can take a while for us to overcome the challenges and embrace the change. One scientist said that information overload is 'confusing and harmful' to the mind. We would be forgiven for thinking that this was made in a recent journal article or blog about the effects of Google. In fact, the author was a Swiss scientist called Conrad Gessner who wrote about the imagined impact of the printing press on society in 1565!

It was ever thus. Socrates famously warned against the practice of writing because it would 'create forgetfulness in the learners' souls because they will not use their memories'. In the eighteenth century, the French statesman Malesherbes campaigned against newspapers, arguing that printed media would socially isolate readers. And the advent of radio and television led to widespread fear that children would stop reading and their exam results would be affected. All of this sounds strangely familiar!

Each generation reimagines the effect of new technology on society, while ignoring the fact that similar concerns were voiced about the very technology it is replacing! But there's a significant difference when it comes to today's technological advances, and that is the sheer pace at which they are developing. Less than 10 years ago, the received wisdom for parents wanting to protect their children was to put the family computer in the living room so that internet use could be easily monitored. Enter Steve Jobs and the rise of the smartphone, and this advice has been rendered obsolete. And it was only just over ten years ago that Jack Dorsey, co-founder of Twitter, sent the very first tweet: 140 characters commenting on

'I'm telling you, this invention will change the world. In a few years we'll be sharing cat photos on a scale you wouldn't believe.'

life, in real time (#IRT), broadcast to the world. Since then, social media has taken the world by storm, and it is difficult to imagine life without it.

Digital technology is advancing at such speed that it is taking time for society to adapt to the changes, but adapt it will. As parents, though, time is a luxury we don't have. Our children need our help and guidance *now*, not in 5, 10 or 15 years' time, when it will be too late.

In my role with Care for the Family, a charity I have worked with over the past decade, I have spoken to thousands of parents at our live events. Time and time again they express concern about their children and the challenge of the digital world. Their main worries are about the amount of time their children spend on screens and the possibility of addiction. Other concerns focus around three core issues:

1. Content: what our children see online
2. Contact: who they are talking to online
3. Conduct: how they behave online

These concerns are wide-ranging and include access to pornography, sexting, the child becoming a victim of online bullying or being the bully themselves, identity theft, awareness of their digital footprint, issues around anonymity, grooming, abuse, gambling, commercialisation of childhood, having no time just to 'be', lack of exercise, and lack of ability to develop face-to-face communication skills.

Reading that list might make many parents forget the benefits and want to run for cover, batten down the hatches, ban all screens forever, and insulate their children in an internet-free cocoon in Outer Mongolia. But even if it were possible, this would not be a good plan. It is too easy to make the internet the scapegoat for the pressures on our children today, and we need to realise that the problem doesn't lie in the internet itself but in the choices we make in using it.

'Unbelievable! Eight weeks and 300 miles on foot
through the planet's harshest environment and they
still have a signal!'

Although, of course, we need to protect our children from danger, our ultimate goal is not to eliminate all risk from their lives (and therefore all opportunity), but to enable them to embrace the opportunities and manage the risks well. In a world of unlimited choices, our role is to equip them to make good ones.

Digital Visitors and Digital Residents

From their earliest days, our job as parents is to teach our children life skills, particularly those that will keep them safe. We teach them how to tie their shoelaces, do up buttons, spell, read, and cross the road. Back-breaking hours spent running behind a bike and holding onto the saddle teaches them to cycle. Even more hours spent waist-deep in the (often chilly and over-chlorinated) water of the local swimming pool results in them being able to swim. We feel we know how to help them develop skills and manage 'real world' risks because we have grown up with those risks and have experience and understanding of them. However, the online world is different, and here is the challenge: even if we are familiar with digital technology and we text, tweet and post on a regular basis, it is unlikely that we will have grown up with digital technology in quite the way that our children have.

Experts have coined the phrase 'digital natives' to describe this generation.[1] They have been born into and have only ever known a media-saturated digital world. The digital language of computers, videos, video games and social media is their native language. In contrast, those of us born a little earlier have had to learn on the go and are sometimes described as 'digital immigrants'. Not everyone agrees with this classification, making the point that there are young people who are not tech-savvy, and there are digital immigrants (born pre-1980) who have been at the forefront of technological development. For our purposes, it is likely that the children of many parents today will have been born into a more technically advanced world than their parents. Of course, parents in their 20s and 30s have more experience than those in their 40s and 50s who are

1 Marc Prensky, 'Digital Natives, Digital Immigrants', *On the Horizon*, October 2001, vol. 9, no. 5: pp. 1–6.

frequently having to play catch-up in a big way and often feel that their children know more than they do. The terminology alone can be confusing. What is the difference between an ISP and an iOS? Is a troll a creature from Norse mythology or something quite different? Are *console* and *monitor* nouns or verbs? Help!

My own children are now adults and live away, but when they come back they still treat our house as *home*. They help themselves to leftovers from the fridge, deposit laundry in the washing basket, and occasionally litter the living room floor with dirty trainers, empty crisp packets, beer cans and dirty coffee mugs. They are *residents*. They know how our house works and what our values are (tidiness clearly not being one of them). However, when friends join them, even if they have been coming to our house for years, they are *visitors*, and as such behave differently. They think differently. They ask before raiding the fridge, wouldn't dream of adding their washing to the pile, and take their trainers (and occasionally even their rubbish) home with them.

This idea of distinguishing between visitors and residents has been used by some researchers[2] to illustrate the various ways people behave online, showing that differences in the use of technology is not just about when you were born. Digital visitors use the internet as a tool, for example, just to get information or check their email. Digital residents see the internet as a more integrated part of their lives, a place to go where they can interact with friends and colleagues or post details of their lives to social networks. As parents, we can try to learn the language by digesting a digital dictionary or mugging up on texting shorthand and discovering what acronyms such as *lol* (laugh out loud), *pcm* (please call me), *t2ul* (talk to you later), *hak* (hugs and kisses) or more importantly, *pos* (parent over shoulder) mean. But if we are visitors we won't ever be as at home in the digital world as those who live there. It involves a different attitude and approach to life.

I will let you into a secret. It is often said that women can multitask. Well, I can't. While I often juggle many tasks, I can

2 David S. White and Alison Le Cornu, 'Visitors and Residents: A new typology for online engagement', *First Monday*, September 2011, vol. 16, no. 9, September 2011. http://journals.uic.edu/ojs/index.php/fm/article/view/3171.

really only focus on one thing at a time. This is in contrast to many teenagers today who are brilliant multitaskers. They appear to have the ability to have several screens open at once while working on a Shakespeare essay, updating their Facebook profile, listening to music, and having a deep and meaningful conversation with a friend – all at the same time. While there might be room for debate on the quality of the essay, there is no doubt that as digital natives they consider this multiscreen task-hopping behaviour perfectly normal.

The online culture has also affected our methods of learning. Instruction manuals with a page count to rival the *Encyclopaedia Britannica* are a thing of the past, and most gismos now come with CD or online instructions. Our son recently learnt how to put new tyres on a bike with the help of YouTube (a stressful scenario for onlookers as it was minutes before he needed to leave the house to catch the ferry for the first leg of an adventure cycling from London to Istanbul). Digital technology delivered the information when he needed it and in the format he needed (and against all odds, he did get the ferry!).

It's very much a generalisation, but digital visitors (i.e. many parents):

- Prefer to talk on the phone or in person
- Use the internet to find out information
- Prefer quality relationships to be face-to-face
- Approach new tasks slowly and in order with printed instructions
- Value privacy

In contrast, digital residents (i.e. most of our offspring):

- Use messaging and social media much more than speaking on the phone
- Use the internet as an important part of building real relationships
- Develop quality relationships online

- Learn using online multimedia information
- Are quite happy to share personal information online

Having checked that list, if you identify more as a digital visitor than as a digital resident, there is no need to feel overwhelmed or ill-equipped to guide your children in this area. The internet is not a tsunami about to engulf us, while we stand helplessly looking on. As parents, we don't need to be computer 'experts', and we certainly don't need to be 'cool' and au fait with every type of digital slang. (The last thing a teenager wants is a 'cool' parent anyway!) However, there are some things we *do* need to know, and there are parenting principles we can implement that are well within our reach.

'Are you posting your dinner to Instagram **again?**'

CHAPTER 2

A RESOURCE
TO EMBRACE

There are undoubtedly dangers (real and imagined) in living in a digital world, but at the outset, let's acknowledge the advantages and opportunities it has already brought us. The benefits for families, as well as the business world, are something we can celebrate, enjoy and make the most of.

My husband, Richard, and I boarded an easyJet flight from Bristol last July. It was our first summer holiday without our children, but apparently unable to change the habits of the last 27 years, we managed to book it in the school holidays. Not only was it more expensive, but the plane was rammed with stressed parents and hordes of small children.

The young mum in the row in front of us seemed to be alternately coaxing and wrestling twin girls into their seats. Amid cries of, 'It's not fair,' she tried patiently to explain that there was only one window seat. The decibel level increased as we took off. It was not proving to be the most restful start to our holiday. However, 10 minutes into the flight, the seat belt sign went off and permission was given for electronic equipment to be used. Within seconds, the fracas in front subsided, and for the entire journey the two girls were glued to a game on a tablet. Heaven! And it's not just holiday flights: in-car consoles have made fractious car journeys in bank holiday traffic with endless games of Hangman and I-spy a thing of the past.

Technology can also be a lifesaver in the home. What parent hasn't breathed a sigh of relief when putting a child in front of a screen during the 'happy hour' – 5 p.m. to 6 p.m. – when blood sugar is at an all-time low, sibling rivalry is at its peak, and the fish fingers are not yet on the table.

The internet has also made education available to many more people – gaining knowledge and information is no longer limited to how many books are in the home. School lessons have been transformed. Harassed parents supervising homework no longer have to trawl through text books and dusty encyclopaedias for information about the cacao bean, volcanoes, the Battle of Hastings or the reproductive cycle of the dragon fly. A click of the mouse on to Wikipedia (which my children tell me is now a legitimate source of reference) has changed everything and opened up new horizons.

There are numerous apps for preschoolers to assist early learning and development – songs, stories and rhymes; games to help them learn colours, numbers and letters; games to encourage tidying up; apps with womb-like noises to encourage sleep; and games that are simply just fun.

Social networks and tools such as WhatsApp, Facebook, Instagram, Snapchat, YouTube, Skype and Pinterest, to name but a few, have facilitated communication between family members and friends. They have given many, young people in particular, a sense of community and belonging. The ability to text and message (a great invention for the introverts among us) has also paid dividends in respect of family communication – including tracking down wandering teenagers. We will look at how involved we can – or even should – be in our teenagers' online lives in a later chapter, but the ability to message them when they are out with friends and establish not only their whereabouts but their expected time home has saved many parents an evening of angst. Our four children are now adults, but in their teenage years when they were out 'roaming', we would ask them to keep their mobile phones with them, turned on and in credit so we could stay in contact if necessary. It was amazing to us how many times they were apparently in the only nightclub or area of Bristol with no signal! Devices are always at the mercy of the user, but the principle of being able to keep in touch is a huge advantage.

To our amazement, my mother, who wouldn't describe herself as tech-savvy, has learnt to text at the age of 82, and being in contact with her children and grandchildren in that way has given her and us an enormous amount of pleasure.

As well as keeping in touch across the generations, software such as Skype or FaceTime enables families to keep in touch across the miles. We have friends who have moved to live abroad. Technology

'No, I'm sure it's fine.
What's the worst that can happen?'

has enabled them to keep in touch with grandparents in a way that just wouldn't have been possible by landline or snail mail. They have Skyped at bath time (the children's bath time, that is!), mealtimes and birthday parties. Stuart (the dad) said, 'It's not the same as being there in person, but we've now made it part of our weekly routine. Mum and Dad feel more part of the children's lives, and we all feel closer as a result.'

Teenagers at a loose end can find hobbies and new interests on the internet. A friend's child has recently found an interest in basketball and can now bore for England on the subject of the leagues. Another child who was struggling academically stumbled across a YouTube lesson on woodcarving and whittling, and this has now become his passion. And still another friend's child is teaching herself the guitar. All this via the touch of a screen.

In many ways, the availability of digital communication serves our teenagers' developmental needs well. Most of our teens will have a mobile phone, and that is the way they prefer to communicate. Out of teenagers who own phones, half send fifty or more texts a day and one in three send a hundred.[3] Most teenagers want to establish their identity, be independent, look cool, and impress members of the opposite sex. Messages on scraps of paper hastily passed along the lunch queue or via a friend are a thing of the past – mobile phones and networking sites have simplified the process! For self-conscious teens, on the day the biggest outbreak of acne has appeared from nowhere, or when a tendency to blush is getting the better of you, social messaging makes this kind of communication much easier.

Many young people have a keen sense of justice. They want to make a difference in the world, and digital technology helps them do that. Sponsored walks, swims and silences have been replaced by initiatives with bigger impact. As teenagers, my children were involved in various fundraising activities and awareness campaigns whose ultimate success was largely due to the viral nature of social media. A couple of years ago, I was presented with a phone and was asked by our youngest to record him having an enormous bucket

---

3 Amanda Lenhart, et al., 'Teens and mobile phones', *Pew Research Center*, 20 April 2010. http://www.pewinternet.org/2010/04/20/teens-and-mobile-phones.

of ice poured over his head for the 'Ice Bucket Challenge'. He then nominated two friends to be subjected to the same treatment and posted it online as part of a viral campaign that raised awareness of motor neurone disease. This same child took part in the 'Cinnamon Challenge' – a dare to eat a spoonful of cinnamon in 60 seconds without having a drink (potentially very dangerous and certainly not to be recommended!). It was a stunt that played into the teenage appetite for fun, risk and adventure and went viral on social media.

Another welcome aspect of digital technology is the benefits it can bring to children and young people with additional needs. At school, devices and software to help pupils with different needs and abilities can help teachers personalise lessons to each child. For children with physical disabilities, technology gives them many opportunities they wouldn't have had: voice adaptive software can help them answer questions without needing to write, e-readers help those with dexterity problems read a book without needing to turn the pages, and the ability to change font sizes and styles can help visually impaired children.

Pippa, the mother of Barney, who has Down's syndrome, told me, 'I love it that Barney, who can't read, can find the music he loves to hear just by looking at YouTube videos. He feels great that he can do this without me helping him.'

Digital technology can also improve communication for children on the autism spectrum and help develop social skills and the ability to learn. Lyn, the mother of a 3-year-old boy with autism said:

After months of using my laptop and Android phone to play games, we decided to get him an iPad. Best. Decision. Ever. Yes, it was expensive, but well worth the money and in just 2 weeks, my son is communicating for the first time with TapToTalk. He is playing games he never had patience/focus/attention for before like match games and puzzles. iPad = Miracle in our house![4]

4 Autism Speaks, 'Technology and Autism'. https://www.autismspeaks.org/family-services/community-connections/technology-and-autism.

Social media sites and gaming can help children with special needs and developmental disorders to communicate and socialise better. One couple commented on the joy, fun, learning and confidence that their two children seem to have gained from gaming: 'Our oldest has anxiety, and gaming was a way for him to fit in with his peers and does make life easier for him. He's very sociable and it's a helpful way for boys especially to chat, while gaming together.'[5] Kyle, who was diagnosed with Asperger syndrome, attention deficit disorder and obsessive compulsive disorder used MySpace and Facebook as a teenager and says that both sites helped him be able to have friends and conversations:

> It's basically just the fact that you don't have to have a person staring back at you with what you're saying ... 2 to 3 years ago and I wasn't able to talk to people face-to-face. Like, this right now, I wouldn't have been able to explain anything. I would have been all shy and weird looking.[6]

Some activities will, of course, remain timeless (reading stories at bedtime, kicking a ball around in the garden, going to the swings and the roundabout in the park, board games and family film nights) and part of parenting in the digital age is to make sure that we include those things for our children. But at the same time, we must be careful not to look back at our own childhoods through rose-tinted spectacles and try to recreate something that is out of kilter with the culture our children are growing up in.

We'll move on to the challenges and potential dangers of family life and digital technology, but as is the case with all aspects of parenting, key to how we handle this is *how* we behave as mums and dads. So what's your parenting style?

---

5 Guardian readers and Matthew Holmes, '"My son overcame his anxiety": parents on how screentime isn't all bad', *The Guardian*, 14 November 2016.
6 Jackie Gerstein, 'Using the Internet and Social Media To Enhance Social-Emotional Learning', *User Generated Education*. https://usergeneratededucation.wordpress.com/2013/02/25/using-the-internet-and-social-media-to-enhance-social-emotional-learning.

CHAPTER 3

PARENTING
STYLES

In the next chapter we will explore one of the big areas of concern for parents: screen time. But before we survey that battlefield, it may be useful to put the coffee on and ask ourselves a fundamental question that will affect how we approach this issue (and many others): *how* do I parent?

John Wilmot, a seventeenth-century poet, has a famous quote attributed to him: 'Before I got married I had six theories about raising children; now, I have six children and no theories.' As a mother of four spirited children, I can identify with his sentiment!

Before our first child was born I was determined to give the important task of parenting my very best effort. I enrolled my husband and myself in antenatal classes, and with a large knitted sock and a rugby ball as a visual aid we were taught all we needed to know about childbirth. We were encouraged to write a 'birth plan'. We could choose a birthing pool, a home birth, or the maternity hospital, and we could select which background music to play and the method of pain relief to use; the possibilities seemed endless. The only fly in the ointment was that son #1 had evidently failed to read the plan or, if he had cast his eye over it, had chosen to ignore it. Three weeks early and making an appearance like an express train, he was having none of it, and this set the pattern of things to come. I was soon to learn that parenting has a lot more to it than blindly following the rules with a guaranteed outcome. The small matters of a determined toddler, stubborn 8-year-old, or defiant teenager keen to make their presence felt, can make life more complicated and unpredictable. Even more confusing is when a normally compliant child surprises us with a little rebellion just to prove that they aren't an easy touch and that we shouldn't take them for granted.

But while there are no guarantees, whatever stage of parenting we are at and whatever the issues, there are some tried and tested principles we can apply that will enable us to parent well.

At our Care for the Family events for parents, one of the sessions that mums and dads find most helpful is when we talk about different styles of parenting. And getting the right style in place will lay a strong foundation as we seek to help our children navigate the digital age.

Experts tell us that there are primarily three styles of parenting. Our particular style will be influenced by our own upbringing as well as by our individual temperament and personality, which will give us a bias. And which style we adopt will affect how we approach setting and maintaining boundaries for our children in the area of digital technology.

At one end of the spectrum is the *authoritarian* parent. This parent can be a perfectionist and likes to be in control. There are lots of rules in the home which are enforced rigidly, with strict punishments for anyone overstepping the line. In this home there will be an exact age limit on when mobile phones, games consoles, tablets and laptops are allowed, regardless of a child's individual maturity or interests. There will be a screen policy with unbending rules covering every minute of the day on where and when children can be online and how many seconds a day they can be in front of screens with no adjustment for age and no allowances for the holidays and special occasions like birthdays. You may well find a rota for charging phones with a labelled, allocated socket for every family member. Authoritarian parents will micromanage their children's online lives even when it's no longer appropriate, insisting that they are their 16-year-old's Facebook friend in order to stay in control.

This sheep and pen picture illustrates the authoritarian style of parenting. The advantage is that it brings clarity; everyone knows what is and isn't allowed, and there is no danger of any ambiguity or misunderstanding. The disadvantage, however, is that children may feel

'I think I've got my parenting theory cracked this time, but we're going to have to have one more child just to make sure ...'

hemmed in and suffocated, with no room for individuality, creativity, spontaneity, independent thought or, more importantly, learning.

I have a friend who parents in this way; her home runs with military precision, rules and regulations. A complex chart on the kitchen wall rivalling an Accident and Emergency admissions board on a Saturday night enables her children to earn tokens for minutes online in return for chores completed to her satisfaction. The rules are fixed, with no discussion or family participation, and no allowance for negotiation.

When our children were younger, I would look at this ordered home that seemed to run like clockwork and find myself comparing it to our more haphazard existence. I'd often feel guilty and, if I am honest, a little envious. This was authoritarian parenting in action, and for a time it seemed to work brilliantly.

But during the teenage years, authoritarian parents may be in for a bit of a shock, and my friend was no exception. While outwardly complying with the rules, as they reach their teens, children in an authoritarian home may begin to harbour a growing resentment at being 'controlled'. They will want to flex their muscles and have the freedom that their friends seem to have. With too many rules and regulations, the authoritarian parent may find to their dismay that their teenagers either push back against those rules or, more likely, vote with their feet, preferring to hang out at friends' homes down the road, where life is more relaxed. Rebellion can sometimes come out later in life – and when it does, it is much more traumatic.

At the other end of the parenting spectrum lies the *permissive* parent. Children with permissive parents may well be the envy of their peers. Their mums and dads are relaxed and laissez-faire, there are very few rules and, even then, few consequences for crossing them. They will have mobile phones, tablets, gaming devices and laptops bought or handed down to them as and when they want them,

irrespective of their age. They will have unlimited screen time, what they are watching will not be monitored, and widescreen HD TVs in their bedrooms may well be the order of the day. The sheep in open country illustrates this permissive style of parenting. Children with permissive parents are free to explore the world wherever it takes them. But while they have plenty of opportunity to forge independence, what they don't have is security. This little sheep looks lost. Boundaries are important – if only to push against – and protective boundaries in relation to the digital world are vital.

The third (and preferred) style of parenting is *assertive*. This is the style to aim for and is illustrated by this picture, where the

sheep has room to explore but can clearly see where the boundary is. Assertive parents know that setting boundaries are important for a child's safety and sense of security, but they will set as few rules as possible. They choose their battles, saying no to the things that really matter and yes to everything else. Clear boundaries for children are set in the context of relationship (it has been wisely said that rules without relationship lead to rebellion) and there is room for negotiation and manoeuvre on both sides. So parents will have guidelines about the appropriate age for their child to have a mobile phone or other device, but they will be prepared to discuss these with them. They will seek to manage their child's safety while not ignoring the peer pressure they may be under – '*Everyone* else has one …'.

Assertive parents will generally allow screen time, but this won't be unlimited – so perhaps no screens at mealtimes or late at night, but with negotiation about this rule in the holidays. This style of parenting is sometimes called 'firm but fair', and is demonstrated by the sheep and pen here. The child can see where the boundaries are and so feels (and is) safe. The gate on the paddock is slightly open, and during the teenage years they can exercise freedom by venturing out of the gate knowing it will still be open on their return.

It is this assertive style of parenting that will best help us achieve our aims for equipping our children to both navigate the dangers and embrace the opportunities of a digital age.

We'll move on now to look at the main challenges and discover how we can manage them well.

'Sorry, guys. This is as far as my chain goes.'

'It's working, honey. I have their attention!'

CHAPTER 4

TOO MUCH
SCREEN TIME?

Eric Schmidt, chair of Google, famously once said, 'If you have a child, you'll notice they have two states: asleep or online.' Parents of teenagers may well recognise that description!

Many parents are concerned about the number of hours that children will spend on screens if left to their own devices, and trying to manage this has become the focus of family life. We may be tearing our hair out as our 3-year-old has a tantrum (aka an iPaddy) on being told his screen time is over. Or perhaps we're going crazy as we attempt to communicate with a teenager whose headphones seem to have become an appendage to his head and whose phone needs to be surgically removed from his hand. The issue is a real battleground in many homes, and the source of many confrontations and rows.

Sometimes our children's screen use may be more covert. I remember a babysitting incident when our children were much younger. My husband and I were running an evening marriage course and needed to be back from work and out of the door again by just after 6 p.m. At 5.45 p.m. Jack, our babysitter, arrived ready to feed our children lasagne, supervise homework and put all four to bed. We returned at 11 p.m. to find that all had gone well apart from the fact that our youngest had been sitting on the loo for the entire duration of the meal. Jack, understandably concerned, had eventually knocked on the door to find out if Henry was still alive. He emerged somewhat sheepishly, I imagine with the loo seat imprinted on his bottom. To Jack's relief, Henry's hour-long sojourn hadn't been due to D and V! He had been totally engrossed playing *Pokémon* on his Game Boy, and despite the allure of lasagne (his favourite dish), he had completely lost track of the time.

Of course, scenarios like this in the home can lead to real conflict, and parents responding to Care for the Family's survey highlighted that the amount of time their children spend on screen is a common concern. One told us: 'It just gets harder and harder as they get older and communication gets harder in general. All comments are seen as criticism and lead to rows. I just can't face it, to be honest.'

A report on children's media use by Ofcom, the communications regulator in the UK, has found that the internet is the top media pastime for UK children – overtaking the television for the first time.[7] Aged 5–15 they are spending around 15 hours online each week, and 3- to 4-year-olds go online for around 8 hours and 18 minutes a week. Over a half of preschoolers use a tablet (with 16% owning their own device). Smartphones are the device of choice for pre- to early-teenage children with one in three 8–11s and eight in ten 12–15s now owning their own smartphone.

These figures are concerning for a number of reasons as we'll see below, but where the rubber hits the road for many parents is the feeling that they are in a continual battle with their children in their attempts to monitor and regulate screen use. Fiona, a mum of four, said:

> We have just come back from a week's half-term, and I am exhausted. Each day was spent using every tactic I could think of to get them off technology and doing something else that didn't involve staring at a screen. I didn't want to spend half-term nagging, but that's what ended up happening. They didn't enjoy it … and neither did I.

Trying to set boundaries around screen use can wear down even the most resilient of parents. Our eldest had an electronic game called *Zelda* that he particularly liked to play, usually just before the evening meal was on the table. Busy families, overlapping schedules, long working days, shift work, homework, after-school activities, and a teenager's burgeoning social life can make coordinating mealtimes a challenge, but we would try to eat together when we could. However, it seemed that whenever the food was on the table,

7 Ofcom, 'Children and parents: media use and attitude report 2016'. https://www.ofcom.org.uk/research-and-data/media-literacy-research/children/children-parents-nov16.

'OK, Son, screen time is over now ...'

son #1 would be at what he considered the most crucial part of the game. Requests to turn it off and sit at the table would be met with pleas of, 'Just 2 more minutes …', 'Just 1 minute more …', 'I'm about to reach the next level, and I can't save it. If I turn it off now, I'll have to start again …' Much research has gone into designing games that keep people playing, and succeeding in moving to the next level was always going to be more exciting for my son than the prospect of supper on the table.

As the debate continued, the spaghetti bolognese would go cold, and my blood pressure would rise. I would like to tell you that we found an easy-to-implement foolproof method of dealing with this, but at the time we didn't. Hindsight is a great thing, and there were definitely some strategies we could have tried that might have reduced the angst. Now a married twenty-something, George was at home recently and rediscovered this childhood game. Just the sound of the catchy tune sent those memories flooding back and started to make me feel on edge!

But apart from the effects of children's screen time on stressed-out parents, what are the dangers to the children themselves? While some can manage on less sleep than others, most parents don't need reminding that there is a direct correlation between (lack of) hours spent asleep and grumpiness in the morning! Children today are sleeping less per night than ever before and below recommended guidelines,[8] and research involving 125,000 children suggests that using devices such as smartphones and tablets at bedtime (within 90 minutes of going to sleep) adversely affects the quality and length of sleep. Given a choice, few children or teenagers would choose sleep over the next game of *FIFA* or *Candy Crush* or a group conversation on Facebook, yet sleep disturbance in children has adverse effects on alertness, concentration, mood, mental health, physical growth and development, and obesity.

Schools are reporting that many children are tired in the morning and schoolwork is being affected by the hours they spend playing

8 L. A. Matricciani, et al, 'Never enough sleep: a brief history of sleep recommendations for children', *Pediatrics*, 2012, vol. 129, pp. 548–556.

electronic games long into the night.[9] Children's sleep patterns are also being affected by the 'always on' culture of social media. One survey[10] found that children were experiencing problems such as not wanting to go to sleep because they were using social media, being kept awake when trying to sleep because their minds were still active, and being woken by their phone bleeping with an alert or message while sleeping. They also reported feeling tired the next day and less ready to learn. Losing track of time when using social media was also highlighted as a factor affecting wider areas of life, including sleep and schoolwork. The availability of many social media applications was identified as a key explanation for this: 'It is routine … going through and checking each one before bed'; 'You forget about the time.'

Another issue to be aware of is the findings of a study at Stanford University,[11] which concluded that heavy media multitaskers have greater difficulty in concentrating and find it harder to ignore distractions and irrelevant information, whereas light media multitaskers are better able to direct and focus their attention on their task goal, control their memory and switch from one job to another. Children also reported that social media use heavily impacted their motivation to complete homework and revise. Not surprisingly, the temptation was hard to resist (for most teenagers, the choice between quadratic equations and checking the latest Instagram feed is never going to be much of a contest!). Comments from participants in the survey included: 'You can use it to procrastinate from schoolwork'; 'I'd rather be on social media than doing homework'; 'Social media takes up revision time.' Children also admitted that social media use in class can distract from learning and can affect concentration, particularly if they feel their phone buzzing. It was estimated between 50–70% of students use their phone during lessons. A challenge for the teaching profession!

Health professionals are aware of the importance of exercise for

9 Hayley Dixon, 'Primary school head forced to warn against gaming and late night TV', *Daily Telegraph*, 11 February 2013, and 'Children are too sleepy for school as three quarters get less than seven hours sleep', *Daily Mail*, 23 March 2012.
10 Fay Poole, unpublished thesis. Newcastle University, 2017.
11 E. Ophir et al, 'Cognitive control in media multitaskers. Proceedings of the National Academy of Sciences', 2009, vol. 106, no. 37, pp. 15583–15587. http://www.pnas.org/content/106/37/15583.

healthy growth and development, and there is growing concern about the lack of physical exercise and levels of obesity among young people. The World Health Organisation has described childhood obesity as one of the most serious public health challenges for the twenty-first century.[12] With nearly a third of children aged 2–15 overweight or obese, it has been described as 'the new smoking'. In fact, if the present trajectory continues, three quarters of the population of the UK are set to be obese or overweight in a single generation,[13] and overweight children are more likely to be overweight adults, with all the accompanying health disadvantages. This is a complex problem, and there are many reasons for it, but the effects of a sedentary lifestyle on 11-year-olds who are spending more time on screens indoors and less time riding bikes, climbing trees and exploring the great outdoors have to be contributory factors.

WHAT PARENTS CAN DO

✓ Be intentional – plan how much time
  they are on screen

It's great to be able to get a half hour of much-needed peace by putting our preschooler or primary age child in front of a screen. But while we catch up with a friend on the phone or do an online grocery order, it's surprisingly easy to discover that 30 minutes has crept into an hour or more. We have simply overlooked how long they have been there. The point isn't that screens themselves are bad – they can be a lifesaver, but they can also be overused as a babysitter.

I would often try to catch up on emails while our children were meant to be doing their homework and, with one thing frequently leading to another, before I knew it their homework had been done

12 World Health Organisation, 'Global Strategy on Diet, Physical Activity and Health: Childhood overweight and obesity', 2004. http://www.who.int/dietphysicalactivity/childhood/en.
13 The Centre for Social Justice, 'Britain is eating itself to death and our plan to fight obesity is woefully inadequate', October 2016. http://www.centreforsocialjustice.org.uk/csj-blog/britain-eating-death-plan-fight-obesity-woefully-inadequate.

'Erm, honey, do you realise it's past midnight …?'

(after a fashion), but I would still be in work mode. While I was making inroads on the inbox they would have seized the moment to play on the Xbox. There wouldn't be anything wrong with the gaming – the issue was that I had no idea how long they had been playing. And while from time to time this was fine, what was not OK was that it was becoming a habit.

In our survey, 70% of parents said that they set some time limits on their child's online activity. How we regulate that time obviously needs to be appropriate for their age – what works for a 5-year-old would clearly be inappropriate for a teenager, but whatever our child's age there are principles we can apply that can prevent screen time becoming such an all-encompassing and recurring issue.

One word of warning is that this will never be a problem we can solve once and for all (unless, as parents, we are totally relaxed about the amount of time our child spends on screen or in the unlikely event they are simply not interested in spending their time in this way). It will be a tension we need to continually manage.

Having some age-appropriate agreed family guidelines for time on screens can be helpful. Each family is different and each child is different, so the important thing is to develop a system that works for you and for your family. What's right for you may be very different from what works for others, so you may need to prepare for your children to frequently bring that annoying character, 'Everyone-else's-parent' into the conversation. ('Everyone else's parents lets them … [fill in the blank].') One parent responding to our survey commented that one of the biggest pressures was: 'Feeling like you can't talk to them about [how much time they are on screens] because you might not be seen to be 'cool' or friendly. Wanting to be their friend instead of their parent.' The fact that 'Everyone-else's-parent' lets them play on their Xbox/PlayStation/Facebook until 11 p.m. on a school night doesn't mean that you have to bow to the pressure to do the same. We do our children a disservice if we try and be their 'best friend'. The truth is that parents have to do and say things that best friends are not prepared to do, and as parents we may have to take a hit in the popularity stakes. No one knows your child like you; nobody loves them like you. They may have many friends, but they only have one mum or dad, so have the confidence to agree some limits that you know work for you and your family.

Involving our children in the discussions and genuinely giving them a voice rather than imposing an arbitrary regime means that everyone is more likely to buy into the agreement. And while it's never too late, the earlier you can start to get good habits in place, the better.

The kind of guidelines you can agree when children are 6 or 7 need to change in the teenage years as they set sail with headphones in their ears and a smartphone in their pocket, on course for increasing independence. While some negotiation with teenagers can take place over screen use in the home, once they are out of the house or at friends' houses it will be up to them to self-regulate the time they spend on screens, so it's worth emphasising to them that with greater freedom comes greater responsibility. And it will be the boundaries that we have put in place over the years and values that we have sown into their lives that will equip them to exercise this freedom wisely.

✓ Decide on your family values

On a camping trip when our children were small, Richard and I were talking with a family friend who was by then grandfather. He told us how he and his family had adopted 'the principle of the three Ds' as a framework for their family values. This was a very simple concept of three behaviours all beginning with the letter 'D' that were out of bounds for their family. They were: ·

- Dishonesty
- Disrespect
- Disobedience

The three 'Ds' are like three sides of a triangle and the family were free to do anything they liked within the triangle but could not cross over it. Each 'D' was something that was important to them as a family:

- Honesty – so there would be consequences for telling lies or other **D**ishonesty.
- Respect – for other people and their possessions – so there were consequences for rudeness, thoughtlessness and **D**isrespect.
- Obedience – so there were consequences for deliberately being **D**isobedient.

Family values are the principles we live by, and it can be helpful to actually think through what our values are. Individual families will have different things that they believe are important, so decide what things ultimately are important to you. We had a number of different values in our family but after hearing about the three Ds from our friend we adopted it and found that although it was a simple formula, it covered almost every eventuality, and when it came to setting boundaries, it wasn't a bad place to start. The point about having family values is that they give us something to aim for and impact how we live in all areas of family life – including the on-screen world.

✓ Use screens to enrich family life

Rather than focussing entirely on policing the amount of time our children are spending on screens, we can allow technology to enhance and enjoy family life together. Our children are grown now and three are married. Since they moved away, we introduced a family WhatsApp group which has increased communication and connection between us in ways we wouldn't have thought possible. Through the WhatsApp posts, I now know more about what is going on in their lives than when we were all living under the same roof! Of course, truculent teens may be reluctant to join in that kind of conversation, but think of ways of using shared technology that works for them such as shared playlists or albums.

It might help also to incorporate screen use in things we might previously have considered a non-screen activity. For instance, one dad told me that family outings with his boys were transformed when he changed his attitude to technology. Instead of telling them to come off the screens and get their coats on to go outside, he adopted a different approach. He encouraged them to bring their phones with them to take photos and to use Snapchat or Instagram or even a GoPro camera to record the afternoon activity.

✓ Draw up a family media agreement

Many families try to draw up house rules for the family about online and screen use called 'family internet agreements' or 'family media agreements', and it's never too early to start! These are simply guidelines in line with your family values that everyone, including parents (here's the challenge!), signs up to. Get some drinks and favourite snacks and make it a fun experience to talk through the issues together with your children. It's obviously easier the younger they are, but even the most combative teenager may cooperate if they think they have a voice and there's something in it for them. You might want to introduce it when your child first begins using technology in the home independently (including video games, tablets, phones, computers and laptops).

If possible, frame it as 'what is allowed' rather than a list of 'don'ts', but with the 'don'ts' remember to think through what the repercussions are if someone steps outside the boundaries. For families with a range of ages of children then the guidelines will need to be on a scale according to age. The agreement isn't a magic bullet and may be too formal for some, but part of its value is simply in sitting down together and talking these things through.

An idea from author Dr Bex Lewis[14] suggests drawing up a three-column sheet with 'Yes, we can', 'Don't like it' and 'Don't even think about it', with the rules potentially moving columns as the children get older. See the appendix for links specifically related to setting family internet agreements, but if you want to create your own media agreement, here are some things you might like to consider:

- How many hours a day can be spent using a computer, tablet, smartphone or playing video games? Does this include or exclude schoolwork?

---

14 Bex Lewis, *Raising Children in a Digital Age: Communicate, Communicate, Communicate*, Lion Hudson, 2014, p. 78.

- Are there different rules for when friends come round/at weekends/on birthdays/holidays?
- What devices can be used and when? At mealtimes? Just before bed? Late at night? Bedrooms or not? (With teenagers, not permitting any use in their bedroom may be unrealistic as they do need some privacy, but the point is not to encourage isolation.)
- Are social media sites allowed, and if so, which ones?
- What information can be or shouldn't be shared online?
- What films/TV programmes can be seen? What is our attitude to adult, violent, or sexual content?
- Are any particular websites off limits?
- Who pays?
- What should your child do if they encounter something scary online or something that makes them feel uncomfortable?

The world is your oyster, but make sure that your children know that the agreement is intended to work *for* your family – a seat belt to keep everyone secure and safe rather than a straightjacket to restrict behaviour. We'll be looking at online safety basics in Chapter 7, and you might like to have a clause saying that following these guidelines is part and parcel of your family's screen activity.

As part of the family media agreement, you may also like to install some software on your family's different devices to limit time online (see appendix for further information). One valiant respondent to our survey said, 'I have programmed the router to switch off at 11 p.m. meaning that no one (including us) has access after that time so as not to show discrimination to the children.'

One family we know agrees that everyone charges their appliances downstairs at night to ensure that they all get a good night's sleep.

✓ Encourage selective TV viewing
In a 24/7 screen world, it is unrealistic of us to expect younger children to have the maturity and self-control to ration their own

viewing. As parents, we can help by setting some agreed guidelines. With TV, we can encourage them to choose specific programmes to view rather than just 'watching television' regardless of what's on, channel hopping, or having it on as background noise. This is so easy to do now as most of the UK's main broadcasters provide a 'catch-up' service, which means that any programme can be time shifted and watched to fit in with the family routine rather than vice versa.

✓ Encourage non-screen activities

When our children were younger, we were given the opportunity to spend a week white-water rafting down a beautiful river and sleeping under the stars at night. We travelled light, and any belongings had to be stowed away in waterproof bags until the evening. We had no mobiles, no screens, no technology! Nothing but the river and the incredible scenery we passed each day. If we'd told our children they would enjoy a tech-free holiday, I doubt they would have believed us, yet all four would now say that week was one of the most enjoyable and fulfilling of their lives. The principle I learnt and tried to apply when we were back home was that if, as parents, we can encourage activities that will catch our children's imagination and sense of adventure, even if they don't seem too enamoured at first, they will find it is possible to have a different kind of fun … even without a smartphone or laptop.

When he was a teenager, one of our sons was excited to be going on a weekend away with his youth club. The kit list came through the week before with essential items to bring – sleeping bag, clothes that you didn't mind getting muddy, a cake, 80s fancy dress – and then there was a PS: 'Please don't bring a phone.' He was incensed. What a 'stupid', 'lame' and 'unfair' rule! What were the leaders thinking? How would they survive? Against all the odds and repeated petitioning from a band of agitated 14-year-olds, the youth leaders held their ground. Returning on the Sunday evening, our son reported that he'd had a 'wicked' weekend and, in a weak moment, even admitted that he hadn't missed his phone.

What I am not suggesting is that parents become self-appointed outward-bound instructors, organising every minute of their children's screen-free time with high ropes/canoeing/coasteering and other risk-taking adventure activities! Not every child will like outdoor activities, and other options are available. My nephew hates any activity involving a ball, but a bank holiday local drama course enabled him to discover a wonderful talent for acting, and he has gone on to study drama at university. Exactly *what* they do isn't important. The principle is to encourage them to discover even a small amount of non-screen activity that they enjoy.

✓ Understand the teenage brain!

In recent years, advances in technology have given us some new information about the changes that occur in the brain during puberty. They are fascinating, and understanding and learning about these changes should be compulsory for all parents of soon-to-be teens! It seems that as well as the incredible burst of brain development that takes place in early childhood, there is an equally significant surge of activity in adolescence. In fact, it's all change as the brain goes through extensive remodelling (it's been described as 'a networking and wiring upgrade') to make it much faster and more sophisticated.

This process means that throughout adolescence, teenagers will get better at balancing impulse, desire, goals, ethics, self-interest and rules – what some psychologists refer to as 'the brakes'. It will result in more complex and sensible behaviour, at least some of the time(!), but at other times, especially to begin with as the brain takes time to adapt, things may not go so smoothly. The two significant parts of the brain that are involved – the amygdala and prefrontal cortex – don't develop in tandem. In practice, the bad news is that many of our teenagers won't get their 'brakes' until well into their twenties. Consequences and making logical common sense decisions come second to taking risks and having a good time. This might shed light on the fact that your 16-year-old seems unable to understand your reasoning when you suggest that FaceTiming their girlfriend until

*'It's not my fault! My prefrontal cortex isn't
fully developed!'*

the small hours the night before their English GCSE exam might not have been the best idea on the planet!

We were going to visit our children's grandparents in Birmingham for a special birthday lunch a few years ago and had made it abundantly clear to everyone (including our boys) that it was a three-line whip and that we needed to be in the car and on the way by 11.30 a.m. at the very latest. (We had a reputation for not arriving on time for family gatherings – one I was anxious to shed.) Our son Ed had been on a sleepover (a misnomer, if ever there was one) the night before, but had promised to be back in good time. At 11 a.m. he texted to say they were all playing *FIFA*, but that he wouldn't be long. 11.15 ... 11.20 ... 11.30 came and went. I texted (IN CAPITALS) to convey my angst and to ask his ETA only to be told, 'Soz – bck asap.' Another phone call elicited the information that the score was Aston Villa 0-0 Man City, and the delay was because they were hoping for a result. We were now going to live up to our (clearly well-deserved) reputation for lateness at those particular family gatherings.

I was not happy – a fact which I lost no time in making my son well aware! Now, years later, I still think I was justified in losing the plot with him, but I might have approached the situation in a more considered way if I had only understood that this was a demonstration – in real time – of the teenage brain's susceptibility for fun to trump logic. They are a work in progress!

When she heard about the teenage brain for the first time, one mum with a 15-year-old said: 'It's such a relief to discover. Not only is it not all my fault, but it's not all his fault either!' Just understanding that our teenagers will approach the consequences of time on screens differently to us makes dealing with the issue a whole lot easier.

CHAPTER 5

NO FACE-TO-FACE
RELATIONSHIPS?

We had family friends round for Sunday lunch. One of the guests was telling us about some writing she was doing on the subject of 'real' relationships. In the course of the conversation she asked our daughter how many friends she had on Facebook. The answer: 1000+. We were open-mouthed – not so much at her reply, but more by the fact that she thought: a) this was normal, and b) these relationships were 'real'. She saw no distinction between 'online' and 'offline' relationships; all these people were her friends whether they were relating to her from behind a keyboard 100 miles away or sitting next to her in an English lesson.

A lively discussion followed that lasted the best part of the meal and reminded the more ancient ones among us of the different way that we understood 'real' relationships. At the end of the conversation we agreed to change our terminology and talk about 'face-to-face' rather than 'real' relationships as, in our daughter's eyes, her 1000+ Facebook friends were every bit as real as the school friends she saw physically every day.

Whatever our thoughts are on the issue of online and offline relationships, communication being carried out via a screen rather than face-to-face clearly has an impact. While Skype and FaceTime may come a close second, they still cannot replace conversation in person with another human being or, more importantly, convey the sheer power of being actively listened to. Many parents are concerned that screen use is inhibiting our children's ability to communicate face-to-face. And it can start so young.

Suzie Hayman and John Coleman's helpful book *Parents and Digital Technology*[15] has a sobering quote:

---

15 Suzie Hayman and John Coleman, *Parents and Digital Technology,* Routledge, 2015, p. 93.

I'm a nursery nurse and one of my colleagues drew my attention recently to a worrying trend. She noticed one child who always looked down at first when you spoke to him, as if when he heard a voice he expected it to come from something in his hands. We realised he's not the only one, and it's the kids whose parents think that iPads and apps on their phones are the answer to a crying child.

– Sandra, mother of two teenagers and a child care professional

If you have preschool children, this conversation may sound familiar:

'Daddy, why can't I have some crisps?'
'Because we haven't got any.'
'Why?'
'Because I haven't done the shopping yet.'
'Why?'
'Because I had too much to do this morning.'
'Why?'
'Because I was busy helping Granny.'
'Why?'
'Because ...'

... and on it goes.

On a good day, a 4-year-old's interrogation worthy of a QC at the Old Bailey may be endearing, but when you are tired and hassled this constant questioning can drive you mad. But annoying as it can be, asking repeated 'Why?' questions is part of a child's natural curiosity and plays an important part in them finding out about the world and their place in it. As they develop language and computer skills, the internet offers every possibility of helping them gather information. They can google and discover answers to the burning questions of life that leave us baffled: 'Why do we never see a baby pigeon?'; 'Why can't I see my eyes?'; 'How much does the sky weigh?'; 'Does God have a beard?' But invaluable as Google and Wikipedia are, digital answers cannot be enough. It is vital that our young children also have the opportunity for a conversation with a real person. And, more importantly, it is vital that there is someone who can give them the value and dignity of being listened to.

One of the most important theories of child development is known as 'attachment theory'. Professor John Bowlby established that strong emotional and physical attachment to a primary caregiver is critical for a child's development.[16] When parents and carers respond to a baby's needs to be fed, comforted, kept warm or stimulated, the baby learns that they are loved and loveable. The baby will learn that if they cry, the parent will pick them up and cuddle them. They will learn that if they smile, the adult will smile back and vice versa. Through these 'bonds' of attachment they build a map of how relationships in life work. The kind of relationship they have with us becomes a template for their future interactions and friendships, so a strong, loving relationship is vital. Without a secure attachment as babies, in later life people can experience feelings of loss and anxiety, poor self-esteem, and an inability to trust others and form positive relationships.

The amazing thing is that the quality of this nurturing relationship actually affects the physical development of the brain. Sobering pictures demonstrate the shockingly smaller and less developed brains of children who have suffered severe neglect compared to those of children who have been nurtured and loved. So a positive attachment experience in early life will affect us throughout the rest of our lives: nurture, as well as nature, plays a vital role in brain growth.

Professionals are not yet certain how screen use at an early age can affect attachment, but it must follow that if a baby spends more time in front of a screen than in eye to eye contact with a parent, the bonds of attachment will not be as strong.

The teenage years present a different challenge when it comes to face-to-face relationships. It was week two of our *Parentalk – Teenagers* course, and a group of parents from the local school had

---

16 J. Bowlby et al. 'The effects of mother-child separation: A follow-up study.' *British Journal of Medical Psychology*, 1956, 29(2), pp. 11–247.

come along, some desperate for strategies to use right away, others keen to get ahead for when the teenage season of parenting arrived! The subject that week was 'communication'. I noticed a mum sitting towards the edge of the group. She looked preoccupied and weary, and she was leaning back in her chair as if collecting her thoughts, grateful for a moment just to herself. The evening began and people started to talk about some of the challenges of communicating with their teenagers – headphones in 24/7 being top of the list.

After hearing some of the other parents' stories, this mum felt empowered to share what was happening in her life. Her husband had died in a tragic accident, and she'd been left to bring up three young girls. Her oldest daughter was 9 at the time of the accident and had been a tower of strength to her through the difficult months and even years that had followed. Bright and chatty by nature, she would light up the room when she came in, usually followed by a group of friends, all chatting, laughing and having fun. Fast forward a few years and things couldn't be more different. The bright, vivacious 9-year-old has morphed into a monosyllabic grumpy teenager. Instead of being her mum's companion and friend, she now won't be seen out with her and makes no attempt to hide the fact that she finds her irritating and annoying.

When she had finished her story, others joined in to relay similar experiences: 'My son won't even look me in the eye'; 'The most I can get out of him is a grunt'; 'She chats away to her friends on the phone, but when I ask her what she wants for tea she bites my head off. I find it so hurtful.' As she listened, the relief on this mum's face was tangible, and she began to cry. She fumbled for a tissue, then looked up and said, 'You have no idea what this evening has meant. Knowing it's not just me has made all the difference in the world. Thank you.'

As we have seen, the teenage years are a time of change and adjustment. When we can't get any response from a 15-year-old who only comes to life when they are on their phone (constantly), it's tempting to lay the blame at the door of social media and technology. But the truth is that some of our communication challenges with teenagers are down to normal adolescent behaviour, possibly exacerbated, but not caused by technology. If your teenager is at that stage at the moment, don't despair – there is hope. As Rob Parsons writes in his book about teenagers, one psychologist likened the teenage experience to the launch of a spacecraft:

With twelve years or so of training behind him, a pubescent boy makes his way to the launch pad. He climbs aboard 'Adolescent One' as his mother and father bite their nails back at Mission Control. The engines roar into life and Darren makes his way into the stratosphere. And then it happens: they lose all contact with the spaceship. Now and again they pick up what sound like grunts, but nobody can decipher them. The years go by, until a whole decade has passed and then suddenly – signals from outer space! Darren's still alive! And, remarkably, he has discovered the power of speech again. His parents rush back to Mission Control just in time to see the live pictures of his capsule bursting into the earth's atmosphere. All their fears are over. Darren is back!

– Adapted from *Teenagers! What Every Parent Has to Know*[17]

WHAT PARENTS CAN DO

✓ Make face-to-face contact with our children

If the way we interact with our children in the early years can actually impact their brain development, it goes without saying that eye to eye contact, smiling, cuddling, playing and tickling will trump time alone in front of a screen every time. Life is busy, and every family has its challenges, but we can try to make the most of those moments while we can.

Waiting for a young mum to vacate a parking space last week, I was amazed to see as she collapsed the buggy that it had a holder for a phone. I wasn't entirely sure if this was for the mum or to keep the baby amused (or perhaps both!). Having baby equipment that

17 Rob Parsons, *Teenagers! What Every Parent Has to Know*, Hodder, 2009.

accommodates digital devices is a useful option (especially if it helps to distract a fractious toddler in the supermarket queue), but not if it discourages face-to-face interaction with our children and prevents us talking and pointing out trees, dogs, caterpillars, pretty leaves, and butterflies on walks to the park.

I was recently visiting an old friend to have a cup of tea together and catch up on life. Noticing the time, I had just got up to leave when she suggested we could have another 20 minutes together if I came with her to collect her children from school. It had been a while since my youngest left primary school, but old habits die hard and waiting outside the classroom felt strangely familiar. However, one thing that was strikingly different was the number of parents on mobile phones, quickly grabbing a few moments to text, chat, or answer an email. At 3.15 p.m. prompt, the doors opened and Class 3 surged into the playground in a sea of blue sweatshirts. One girl in particular caught my attention; she was waving her painting and calling, 'Mummy, Mummy! Look! Look! LOOK!' This mum was dressed in a black suit and stiletto heels and was engaged on the phone on what seemed to be a work call. To her credit, one look at her daughter's eager face made her decide that matters of company budgets and strategy could wait – there was more important business to attend to. She ended the call, bent down (quite a feat in those heels), cupped her daughter's face in her hands and said, 'Darling, that's a lovely painting. Tell me all about it.'

It's not just 5-year-olds that need face-to-face contact. Teenagers need it just as much but *on their terms*, that is, at the most inconvenient times of the day or (more usually) night! Be alert. It's certainly not always easy, but we need to be ready to grab what scraps of face-to-face communication we can. It will be worth it.

We can seize moments for real conversations during the everyday routines of family life such as when we're with our children in the car (a great one for teenagers because there's no escape!), on the school run, and especially at mealtimes. Ikea recently reported a drop in sales of dining-room furniture as many families now prefer to have meals on laps in front of the TV rather than sitting round a table together. I remember trying hard not only to eat together as a family when we could, but to have mealtimes as a screen and mobile-free zone, even when our children's friends were round. An opportunity to encourage conversation was a game we played called 'High/Low' when we would take it in turns to tell each other the high and the low of our day. The children didn't always cooperate, but just occasionally we would hear of a goal scored in a football match, a falling out in the playground, a good mark for a history essay or a mean Facebook post – things I doubt we would otherwise have found out about.

Everyday moments of communication may be lean in the teenage years (so take hold of them when they come your way!), but it's also possible to create them intentionally. At Care for the Family's parenting events, I often talk about a routine that Richard and I developed when our children were quite young. In order to have some one-to-one time with each child, one of us would take one of them out to Tesco for breakfast on a Saturday morning. With four children, it meant they got a turn once a month, and they could choose which of us they wanted to go with. After a while, as I waved my husband off for yet another breakfast, it began to dawn on me that he seemed to be the companion of choice – I hardly ever got to go! Why didn't they want to come out with me? Was I not a fun mum? Feeling a little insecure, I made some enquiries. This is what I discovered: breakfast with me involved Weetabix, smoothies and toast, but breakfast with Richard included chocolate eclairs and Cheesy Wotsits all downed with a bottle of coke. I realised at that moment that this exercise wasn't about healthy eating. Important as their five-a-day was, it could be overlooked on Saturday mornings in order to create a fun time that they looked forward to and that gave both them and us the opportunity to talk and to listen! The conversation would rarely be deep and meaningful. We would chat about the latest *FIFA* game (always a struggle for me) or hair braids (more of a struggle for Richard), but, especially in the teenage years, there were some precious moments of screen-free connection where we could chat about the important things of life and allow space for them to share their hopes, their fears and their dreams.

Those Saturday morning visits to Tesco have laid a foundation in our children's lives. They are now in their 20s and living away, but they will still seize the chance if they are home to take one of us out for breakfast!

✓ Encourage our children to give others face-to-face contact

As well as creating face-to-face communication with our children, we can encourage them to give it to others. If visitors come to the house, it's not a bad idea to insist that our children press the pause button on their device – just for a couple of minutes – to look up, give eye contact, and say hello (even if they really don't appreciate Aunty Hilda who wafts in smelling of lavender, insists on that awkward kiss and tells them how much they have grown). It is one small way that gives the message that face-to-face communication really does matter.

✓ Encourage opportunities for one-to-one relationships through online activity

Let's not ignore the fact that the digital world gives children the tremendous opportunity to engage with others of the same age whether at home with siblings, at a friend's house, or at school. Collaborative learning at school gives them the opportunity to work with others while researching a homework project, preparing a presentation with friends online or making a film. Even playing games involving more than one player can help develop their communication skills.

One of the advantages of living in a student city when our children were younger was the ready supply of willing babysitters. A procession of hungry students were only too pleased to have an evening in a warm house and some home cooking in exchange for looking after our tribe. The children themselves had their favourites (one was blacklisted after rationing them to one small slice of chocolate cake and insisting they switched channels and joined her in watching *The Antiques Roadshow*). Top drawer by a long way was an engineering student called Charlie. Charlie wasn't interested in *The Antiques Roadshow*, and he let them eat chocolate cake until they felt sick, but best of all he played computer games with them. They would be desperate for us to go out just so he could come round.

'Help! My mum's put the childlocks on and is trying
to have a conversation with us!'

Seeing how popular Charlie was, Richard and I tried to follow suit and played computer games with our children as well. But we were hopeless and while they humoured us, it wasn't much fun, for them or us. I finally came to terms with the fact that I was never going to be as dexterous as our children on the PlayStation (although I gave them a run for their money on the Wii). But we discovered that a close second to actually playing the games with them ourselves was to be interested in what they were doing and talking face-to-face about what was going on. Being involved in that way in their screen activities kept our channels of communication open.

'**Wow**. *Well done, Dad. You won* **again!**
You're **so good** *at computer games.*
I don't know **how** *you keep beating me so easily ...'*

CHAPTER 6

'EVERYTHING THEY DO IS ONLINE!'

It was a Friday morning and I was in the doctor's waiting room. Every seat was taken. I imagine that most of us were in the same predicament – needing to visit the GP 'urgently' with a minor ailment which wouldn't, in our opinion, wait until after the weekend. A message flashed on the screen to apologise that appointments were running late. In that moment, almost every person in the room put a hand in their pocket or dived into their bag and produced a mobile phone. There was an unsaid agreement; if we were going to have to wait, we would make the most of every second. I checked my family WhatsApp group and others caught up on emails and messages while the child next to me proceeded to play *Angry Birds* on his mother's phone (I was impressed – he was obviously well practiced!). As I waited for my turn, I reflected on the hours I'd spent waiting in that room over the years with the range of ailments that beset young families, and, in the absence of *Angry Birds*, the fidgeting and wrestling that would take place while waiting for our name to be called.

But however welcome apps and games are in occupying fractious children in waiting rooms, the availability of 24/7 entertainment does mean that our older children are seldom offline. (And if they are, it is probably because the battery on their phone has just died!) With young children, imaginary games using whatever props are around them and make-believe stories encouraging creativity and adventure can all too easily be usurped by the beckoning swipe of a screen.

Perhaps more importantly, the 24/7 'always on' culture means that our children have no time to be 'bored' or even just to 'be'. A newspaper article I read recently encouraged its readers to 'Lean into boredom and not your smartphone screen.'[18] The truth is that if we can learn to embrace boredom rather than reaching for our phone or tablet in every idle moment, we can discover more about ourselves and the world around us than we would think possible, and we can encourage our children to do the same.

At least once during the school holidays one or more of my children (and even, horror of horrors, all four of them) came out with the words that cause a sinking feeling in the heart of every parent: 'I'm bored!' It's so easy to respond to this by springing into action and providing some form of activity – digital or otherwise, to keep them fully entertained.

Perhaps it's because we feel like we're failing them if they are bored, or that boredom is a 'problem' we have to solve. But psychologists say that quite the reverse is true: 24/7 activity can be counterproductive, and far from being a bad thing, unstructured time is important for a child's healthy development.

In his infinite wisdom, Winnie the Pooh once said, 'Don't underestimate the power of doing nothing.' Wise words from a bear! But many of us lead busy lives; we have family responsibilities, demanding jobs, endless to-do lists, and can't imagine the luxury of being able to do nothing. More and more of us are growing accustomed to living in the fast lane; it has become a way of life. 'Busy' is worn as a badge of honour. We tweet in the supermarket queue and catch up on emails while waiting for the kettle to boil, but the only problem is that those we live with, especially our families, also get caught up in the vortex.

As parents, we are the pacesetters in the home. Our children take their cues from us and begin to live 'busy' lives themselves. Hard as it is, we may need to take a long look at our priorities and make some tough calls. Do we fill our children's week 24/7 with activities that educate and entertain? Or do we allow them time to be bored and to switch off from the bombardment of the outside world? What example are we setting them with regard to our screen activity? Do we allow ourselves time to dream, time to imagine,

18 Gayatri Devi, 'Boredom is not a problem to be solved', *The Guardian*, 28 September 2015.

'I really don't know where you find the
time to put your "busy" badge on ...'

and time to discover gifts and talents? We don't have to be budding Picassos, emerging J. K. Rowlings, or embryonic Mozarts to benefit from boredom; it seems that just letting the mind wander is beneficial for everyone's emotional well-being. Research has shown that if we engage in some low-key undemanding activity without concentrating on anything we are much more likely to come up with creative ideas[19] (which may explain why I have all my best ideas in the shower!).

Writer and actress Meera Syal relates how she spent the school holidays staring out of the window and doing various things outside her usual sphere – like learning to bake cakes with the lady next door. Out of boredom, she began writing a diary and she attributes this to her writing career: 'It's very freeing, being creative for no other reason than that you freewheel and fill time.'[20]

Unstructured time gives children the opportunity to explore ideas and interests, imagine, invent and create. If our reaction to 'I'm bored' is to fill their time with activities, they may never learn to identify and respond to inner 'calls' that can develop the interests and passions that make life so meaningful. Whether it's baking, drawing, cycling, making a short film, helping out at an animal refuge, or crafts, their interests and talents can only develop when we give our children the freedom and space to pursue them.

WHAT PARENTS CAN DO

✓ Check the pace you are setting your family

It's worth asking ourselves what pace we are setting in our home. Is it sustainable and, more importantly, does it give our children time and space just to 'be'?

When our children were at primary school we found that without realising it, we had stepped onto a fast-moving conveyor belt of after-school activities: Brownies, Cubs, swimming, football, judo, guitar.

19 *The Anatomy of Rest*, 'What happens when your brain wanders?', BBC Radio 4, broadcast on 20 September 2016. http://www.bbc.co.uk/programmes/p048gx4t.
20 T. Belton, 'How kids can benefit from boredom', University of East Anglia. https://www.uea.ac.uk/research/blogs-and-comment/how-kids-can-benefit-from-boredom.

Most of these involved a car journey in rush hour traffic, and then there was homework and music practice added into the mix. It was a way of life we had slipped into – and it was unsustainable. Wise words from a friend enabled me to regain a sense of perspective, and the following term I cancelled almost all of those activities. It didn't give me the 'mother of the year' award, but in hindsight it was one of the best parenting decisions we made. The frantic rhythm of our family life settled down.

And, of course, part of setting the pace in family life is not just about our children's activities but our own. Parents are often worse at filling gaps with digital activity, and we can actively set a visible example of valuing offline activity or downtime.

✓ Give your children some space

When our four were of primary school age, the often wet summer holidays would sometimes feel very long, and I would run out of ideas to keep them entertained. A friend with children the same age had a different approach to the challenge. It seemed that every day she would be packing up a picnic and going swimming or heading off to an adventure park, the cinema, a castle or museum. Her schedule for the children was packed and her energy amazing. With the very best of intentions, she would give me leaflets about activities in the area and encourage me to plan ahead like she did.

Feeling I was letting our children down by not following suit, I remember packing up a picnic one day, loading the car and setting off. The day wasn't without incident! The highlight for the boys (although it reduced our daughter to tears) was when I was stopped by the police for entering a yellow box before the exit was clear. Within minutes of our arrival there were a series of unwelcome events: son #1 pushed his brother into a pile of stinging nettles (no tube of antihistamine in sight in our car, but my friend, of course, had a first aid kit handy); my youngest filled his nappy on a little train miles from the car park asphyxiating the rest of the carriage; we had to queue for hours for the face-painting (worth the wait for the lion but not the butterfly); and all four voiced their extreme disappointment that our picnic was inferior to the spread my friend had laid on. Despite all this, we had to admit later that it had been a fun day (and one for the memory banks!), but not one that I had the energy or resources to arrange every other day of the holidays. I looked at my friend's action-packed regime and felt so guilty, and there were double measures of guilt the following week when my children declared they were … bored.

I've now come to see things a little differently. As we've discussed, boredom isn't all bad – in fact it presents a wonderful opportunity. If I have grandchildren I will encourage their parents to make space for boredom. Parents have a role to play not just in making that space, but in then not being too hasty to rush in with ready-made solutions. If our children are younger we may need to provide some materials (some sticks, a ball of string, a rug, a bag of flour, a balloon – the simpler and messier the activity the better!).

If they are initially stuck for ideas we can always give them a challenge to get them going, something to encourage curiosity and imagination – a scavenger hunt, an obstacle course, a story to perform, a den to make, a song to sing. If we allow our children time to be bored the options are endless.

Teenagers too will benefit from taking a break from the 'always on' stimulus of external entertainment and the need to fall back on screens to keep boredom at bay. This is undoubtedly more difficult to manage as they get older, but just creating the space for it to happen is a start. We all tend to be 'busy' and we all use the 24 hours allocated to us each day with none left over. The key is in what we choose to be busy with. And if we can choose wisely, not just for us but for our children, our whole family can discover the benefits of slowing down and creating the space just to 'be'.

'It's Daddy's TV time now – I've been bored at work all
day. Off you go and be bored in your bedroom.'

'It seems more like **ANTI**-social media to me.'

CHAPTER 7

SOCIAL MEDIA, IDENTITY, AND DIGITAL FOOTPRINT

Social media plays a big part in a child's life today – especially for our teenagers who use it to play games, share photos and pictures, message each other, chat via video and meet new people. It's fun and creates opportunities for our children to connect with each other, and take part in many positive things online.

As parents, our role is not to deny our children these opportunities, but to protect them from the possible negative aspects, and using the networks' own guidelines regarding age limits is something that can help us. Even though most social networking sites have a minimum age of 13, 50% of all 11- and 12-year-olds have an account.[21] Perhaps this is because some parents feel that age-restrictions don't matter too much, but the NSPCC reported that almost a quarter of 11- and 12-year-olds using social media last year said that they'd had an upsetting experience during the previous year:[22]

These experiences range from trolling [when someone posts inflammatory, disruptive, abusive or off-topic messages online to provoke or upset you] to online stalking to being asked to send a sexual message. While most of these children were able to recover from what they encountered quickly, around one fifth felt upset or scared for weeks or months after the incident occurred. A fifth of those who experienced something that upset them told us that they experienced this every day or almost every day. Furthermore, the evidence indicates that these upsetting and frightening experiences are not merely an extension of what is happening in the playground. Worryingly, children reported that over half of these experiences were

21 'Keeping children share aware', NSPCC. https://www.nspcc.org.uk/preventing-abuse/keeping-children-safe/share-aware.
22 C. Lilley, et al, 'The experiences of 11–16 year olds on social networking sites', NSPCC, 2014. https://www.nspcc.org.uk/globalassets/documents/research-reports/experiences-11-16-year-olds-social-networking-sites-report.pdf.

caused by strangers, people they only knew online, or they did not know who caused it.

It's worth remembering that in having their own social networking profile, our child will not just have access to a particular site's content – they will be invited to sign in via that profile to other sites.

It has always been the case that an important part of growing up involves young people flexing their muscles, discovering who they are, and establishing their identity as separate from us, their parents. But the difference for our children today is that they must do this in a media-saturated world that not only judges them on what they look like but presents a distorted view of reality. Society feeds them the lie that they are what they own, their value is in what they look like, and their worth lies in the number of likes they have on Facebook. Mixed with the consumer pressure to buy, buy, buy, these messages are a potent cocktail for our teenagers.

The selfie culture reflects one aspect of this pressure, encouraging our children to constantly document who they are through photographs: 'I post, therefore I am.' It's all too easy for them to end up comparing their behind-the-scenes life with everyone else's showreel on social media and the pressure to look perfect (with a six-pack/thigh gap/'hot dog' legs/tiny waist/big bottom/big chest/ doleful eyes) is immense. This is combined with the stress of exams, and the need to be liked and accepted, to have a boyfriend/girlfriend, and to get a job.

The online world gives young people an unprecedented opportunity to establish their identity. They can experiment with new ideas, causes, and memes all behind the safety of the screen. But as well as allowing them to define and build their identity, it also allows them to *redefine* it – to write a new script. There is the possibility to tweak and amend their social media identity, or even recreate it, until it bears little relation to real life.

Hero Douglas, a 17-year-old musician, said this:[23]

23 C. Midgley, 'Social media and the trouble with teenage girls', *The Times*, 23 August 2016. http://www.thetimes. co.uk/article/social-media-and-the-trouble-with-teenage-girls-3nctqt3zm.

I don't post photos of me weeping with mascara running down my face after I've fallen out with a friend or screwed up a musical performance. I publish a constant stream of highlights of my life. And, of course, my friends put up similar images that illustrate their brilliant lives. It's mostly the highlights we share, not the sad bits when we feel lonely, unattractive, stupid and a failure.

And here lies the danger: a gap develops between real life and our Instagram identity, and as the gap increases it fuels our anxiety that even if we get lots of 'likes', we won't be able to live up to the 'self' we have created.

Psychologist and author Linda Papadopoulos comments:

We start to view ourselves in the third person. We effectively step outside ourselves and become observers of our own lives, constantly wondering how we measure up in the eyes of others, ready to edit who we are in order to conform or please.[24]

After school one Friday evening, 15-year-old Daisy was at her friend's house with some girls from school. She was immature for her age, shy and not as confident as the other more sophisticated and savvy girls. They'd been trying on outfits and taking selfies when one of them suggested they all upload their photos to Facebook's 'Hot or Not' app to see what would happen. It's a rating site that allows others to go on and click whether they rate the person in the photo as 'hot' or 'not'. Daisy's heart sank. She was terrified to take part but even more frightened of not being seen as part of the group, and so, reluctantly, she agreed. It wasn't the best photo of herself, she knew that, but secretly she hoped she'd get a good score and that this would help her feel more confident with her peers. Later that evening, she plucked up enough courage to check the app. Her heart sank even more as she saw the results. She knew it was stupid,

24 Digital Parenting Magazine, Issue 4. https://www.vodafone.com/content/dam/vodafone-images/parents/assets-2016/pdf/Digital_ParentingMagazine_Issue_4.pdf.

but she couldn't help checking every few minutes, hoping against hope that her score would have increased. It was well after midnight when she finally fell asleep, her pillow wet from her tears.

It's a tough world out there for our children as evidenced by recent statistics on their mental health and well-being. The Office of National Statistics reports that one in ten young people have a mental health problem[25] – the equivalent of three in every classroom. A larger group of young people are not diagnosed with a specific mental health issue, but are recorded as experiencing low levels of well-being. Just under one in five young people have high levels of anxiety, for example.[26] A new government survey shows that there is a 10% increase since 2005 in the number of girls aged 14–15 with anxiety or depression, but on a more positive note, there is less experience of depression among young teenage boys.[27]

Overall, it's a worrying trend and of course the causes are numerous – the pressure of exams, high expectations, pushy parents, long-standing illness or disability, parental conflict or divorce,[28] and friendship issues, to name just a few. One of the concerns of parents is whether social media use is contributing to the problem. The evidence of a link is inconclusive at present; however, the Office for National Statistics data does suggest there is a correlation, though not necessarily a causal link. Just 12% of children who spend no time on social networking websites have symptoms of mental ill health, but this rises to 27% of those who are on the sites for 3 hours or more a day.[29]

Anecdotally, however, there is more evidence of the harmful effects, particularly on girls. Eighteen-year-old Keira, who has suffered from severe depression, self-harming and eating disorders since the age of 13, described the pressures she experienced coming from two directions: exams and social media: 'You're pressured not only into having the looks and weighing a certain amount; it's

25 The Office for National Statistics, 'Mental health of children and young people in Great Britain, 2004'.
26 Office of National Statistics, 'Measuring National Well-being: Insights into children's mental health and well-being, 2015'.
27 Department of Education, 'Longitudinal Study of Young People in England cohort 2: health and wellbeing at wave 2', July 2016.
28 Ibid.
29 Office of National Statistics, 'Measuring National Well-being: Insights into children's mental health and well-being, 2015'.

also [about] getting the perfect grades.'[30] She believes that social media can certainly exacerbate feelings of worthlessness, even if it doesn't actually cause them. 'It's all about how many likes you get.' According to Marjorie Wallace, of the mental health charity Sane:

> One of the problems is the way in which 24/7 exposure on social media can have a potentially destructive effect on issues such as self-esteem, body image or sex. Young people can find themselves damned if they do take part and damned if they don't, as they risk becoming isolated from their peers.[31]

Instamodel Hailey Baldwin admits that the main part of her brand is social media – and it's interesting that she came off it for a month last year saying that she needed some space.

> Sometimes I feel it's too much. If I could have kept off it longer, I would have but I had to post things for work. From the moment I turned it off to the day I turned it back on, I was free … It definitely does something to the soul … There are times when I feel depressed or anxious and a big part of it comes from that. If we didn't have social media, we'd have a weight lifted off our shoulders. I try to make my Instagram more about work than not.[32]

But let's not throw the baby out with the bathwater. Using social media is fun for many, and both social media, and the internet more widely, have been shown to benefit young people with mental health problems because they can communicate with others who are having the same experiences and join online support groups. The connection with mental health and social media will continue to be a vital area of research.

---

30 C. Midgley, 'Social media and the trouble with teenage girls', *The Times*, 23 August 2016. http://www.thetimes.co.uk/article/social-media-and-the-trouble-with-teenage-girls-3nctqt3zm.
31 *Ibid.*
32 Harriet Walker, 'Hailey Baldwin: I selfie therefore I am', *The Times*, 11 March 2017.

Digital Footprint

Digital natives tend to be more relaxed than digital visitors about sharing personal information online. Whether it's photos, selfies, videos, opinions, or likes and dislikes, they see it as a natural extension of their offline lives and the boundaries for each are blurred. As they build their online identity they will be building a unique 'digital footprint'.

And what we can see on the screen of our own or other people's identities is just the tip of the iceberg. In completing the 'If you were a dog, what breed would you be?' online quiz, what seems like harmless information may in fact give data mining companies all kinds of personal information about us that can be stored and enable us to be identified. Google may give us information, but it is not for free – in return they receive information about us which they can use in a variety of ways.

In his first lecture at medical school, a friend's son was warned that future employers may check applicants' social media presence at interview. Rants about animal testing, hunting, the environment, politics or any other issue, pouting poses in changing rooms, recordings of high jinks stunts, photos of exam celebrations, drinking games at the rugby club dinner ... anything and everything, discreet and indiscreet, would be there (or discoverable) for those who wanted to see. These future members of the medical profession were sobered as they realised that if they weren't careful, the hoped-for string of letters after their names might also come with another less welcome tag.

In a moment we are going to look at some practical things we can do, but first of all let's lay a foundation on which these can be securely built: unconditional love and acceptance. There is one question on the lips of every child and every teenager – in fact, every human being – on planet earth. It's a question that goes to the very heart of human existence: 'Am I loved?'

In a society that screams at our young people, 'I will love you if you are pretty/handsome/slim/clever/popular/good at sports ...', as their parents we have an incredible opportunity to tell them a different story. We have it in our power to build a family where our children know that they are loved not for what they look like and not because of the number of likes or retweets they have secured, but simply for who they are. They are being drip-fed the message that image is everything, but we can counter that by showing them that our love for them is unconditional – that we love them, value them, and accept them … hot or not.

One of the most effective ways of making a child feel accepted is through what we say. A wise proverb says that our words have 'the power of life',[33] and as parents we can speak life to our children through things that we say that will build their confidence and self-esteem. And it can be in the simplest of ways. When my daughter left school, she got a job as a lifeguard at the local gym. The first week didn't go well. The other staff were cliquey and she had to deal with some complaints and some difficult customers. She was on the verge of giving up, and to encourage her I put a Post-it note in her bag which simply said, 'Charlotte, we think you're great' along with a smiley face. I thought no more about it; she carried on with the job, went travelling for 6 months, and then went off to university. About 18 months later, we were at home and Charlotte asked me to grab her bag and get a receipt out of her purse. As I looked for it, I stopped dead in my tracks. There alongside the receipts and lists was that Post-it note. She had kept it all that time and even taken it around the world with her. Positive, kind, affirming words can build our children's self-esteem and sometimes be literally life-giving.

WHAT PARENTS CAN DO

✓ Find out what it's all about ... and join in

While we don't need to become experts, it is worth finding out about the social media platforms our children are using if we aren't already familiar with them. Even if we will never be avid users ourselves of Facebook, Instagram, Snapchat or whatever social media our children favour, we can still set up an account so we know how it all

33 Proverbs 18:21, NIV.

works, can talk to our children in an informed way, and engage with them online. Above all, be sensitive. They may not appreciate your Snapchat stories in quite the same way as you do!

✓ Teach your children the online safety basics

The online safety basics are as key for us to teach our children today as crossing the road, not opening the door to strangers, or learning to swim. With younger children, we can talk to them about what they share and explain what 'personal information' is, and why it's important to keep this private. Warn them that not everyone may be who they say they are online, so it's best to speak only to people they know. Rather than giving them a long lecture all at once – which they will probably not take in – have short conversations over a period of time. Help them to choose usernames that don't reveal private information and make sure there are privacy controls on information-sharing apps.

Safety guidelines

- Never give out your real name.
- Never give out your address or telephone number.
- Never tell anyone where you go to school.
- Never agree to meet anyone from a chatroom on your own. Only meet them in a public place with one of your parents or another adult. If they are genuinely who they say they are, they will be happy to do this.
- Tell an adult if someone makes inappropriate suggestions to you or makes you feel uncomfortable or upset online.

Danger signs

- If someone tries to insist on having your address or phone number.
- If someone emails you pictures which make you feel uncomfortable and which you would not want to show to anyone else.
- If someone wants to keep their chats with you secret.

- If someone tells you that you will get into trouble if you tell an adult what has been going on.
- If someone wants you to email them pictures of yourself or use a webcam in a way which makes you feel uncomfortable.
- If someone shares information with you and tells you not to tell anyone else about it.
- If someone wants to meet you and tells you not to let anyone know.

If you find any of these danger signs it's important that you tell your parents or another adult.
– Adapted from advice by Bullying UK, Family Lives[34]

✓ Put parental controls in place

If young children are in the house, we tend to put things like knives and bleach out of reach. When our children were little, we put the carving knives on a high shelf, and it occurred to me the other day that as our youngest is now 6'3", at 5'1" I am the only person who has to climb on a chair to reach them! In the same way, we can put age-appropriate external safeguards in place to protect our children from digital harm. To do this effectively, we need to be smart, keeping ahead as far as possible – and that means getting informed and taking action.

With multiple devices, it's not enough just to set parental controls on the computer; we also need to think about smartphones, games consoles (which many parents don't realise can connect to the internet), tablets and any other gismos in the home. Some may find this complicated to navigate at first, but it is essential that we don't bury our heads in the sand, leaving them to their own devices.

Parental controls are software tools that you can install on home broadband, phone or tablets, laptops or games consoles to filter the content your child sees when searching online (although this may not always be useful and can block sites they *do* need to access, for school projects, for example). They will also allow you to set time limits for when your child can go online and how long for, and block

34 Bullying UK, 'How to stay safe online'. http://www.bullying.co.uk/cyberbullying/how-to-stay-safe-online.

programmes they are not old enough for. Some companies provide software to filter both computers and phones, which works at home and when out and about.

And, of course, age restrictions for the use of social media are your friend, and there are privacy controls on social networks that you can make sure are in place. Go to your broadband provider for details about the service they offer and see the appendix for useful sites.

Controls obviously need to be age-appropriate – what is necessary to protect a 10-year-old is likely to be over-restrictive for a 16-year-old – but used wisely, they will go a long way to keeping our children safe.

However, there is a caveat. Filters and parental controls are essential but, like contraception, they will never be 100% effective. And, anyway, tech-savvy kids are adept at finding a way round the most robust of filters. When our children were young we were staying for the weekend with some old friends from college days. Having got all the children into bed for the night, we settled down with a glass of wine to watch a film only to discover that their 7-year-old had cracked their internet password and set it to block parental access! Resetting it was beyond the competence of his parents – and us – so they had to wake him up and ask him to do it. I recall that our friends had rather a sense of humour failure on that occasion and didn't find the escapade quite as funny as we did.

✓ Find suitable sites and apps
Don't ignore age guidelines for games, apps and social media – they are there for a reason. See the appendix for organisations who review and recommend sites that are appropriate for children at different ages.

✓ Talk to older children about the long-term effects of everything they do online
If your child is at the younger end of the teen years you might try sitting down together and looking for them online using different search engines to check their name or nickname and search Google

images. Does anything include private information like their school, address or phone number? How are they representing themselves through photos, likes and comments on social media?

Remind your children that everything they post builds their reputation, and what goes online, stays online. It's important that they use privacy settings on social media and block unwanted contacts, but none of these safeguards are fool-proof, and it's difficult to keep things private – friends can pass on photos or messages and accounts can get hacked. Encourage simple common sense to help them manage personal information and particularly to develop an online reputation that they would be proud of. Research shows that 35% of employers use social media to screen potential employees.[35] Perhaps a good test when they are about to post something is to ask themselves: 'Would I want my Granny to see this?'; 'Would I want this to be on a poster for my family, friends and the whole school to see?'; and 'Would that post take some explaining at a job interview?'

What we do online can also affect others, of course, so talk to them about the old adage 'Do as you would be done by' – or, in other words: be kind. Even if we are not intentionally mean, it can be easy to post something we think is 'funny' at the time, but ends up causing hurt or embarrassment to our friends or family.

✓ Be a good role model

As well as being a good role model when it comes to on-screen time and face-to-face relationships, as parents we can be a good example in the way we use social media, making sure that we never post anything ourselves that we wouldn't want them to see. For many of us that may mean taking a good long look at our Facebook account and seeing how much we 'overshare' – particularly our children's photos. It's worth thinking about the fact that babies today will have a digital footprint from the moment Mummy, Daddy, Auntie or Granddad post online that first photo of them as a newborn.

---

35 Internet.matters.org., 'Online reputation'. https://www.internetmatters.org/issues/online-reputation.

WHEN THINGS GO WRONG

If we discover our children have posted something online that they regret, we can reassure them, listen and tell them that we'll do everything we can to help sort it out. Above all – and as hard as it may be! – it's important to try to stay calm, particularly if they are very upset. Ask them to tell you exactly what has happened and then, as a first response, ask or help them to delete the post as quickly as possible.

If someone has posted something upsetting or offensive about our child, and they refuse to take it down when asked, we can help report it to the website concerned. It doesn't guarantee that the content will definitely be removed, but the site does have an obligation to do so if it is in breach of their rules. See appendix for useful websites that can help in this situation.

'Tag Granny in this photo.
She'd love to see this!'

CHAPTER 8

PORNOGRAPHY

Our house is next to a little path that goes down to the local school – our four children went to it when they were young. Every morning, a procession of mums with buggies, some dads with 2-year-olds on their shoulders, and school children in bright blue sweatshirts dragging book bags behind them, walk past on the way down to the school. At 3.30 p.m. the procession returns. It all takes me back to when our children were young, and sometimes I feel a sense of sadness that that season is over. But as I've watched these little ones lately, another emotion has overwhelmed me.

I feel angry. Angry that we have sleepwalked into allowing unbelievable dangers to spread into society and threaten children's lives. The fact is that within 3 or 4 years, these infants will be able to download the pornography of the world – because even if they don't have a smartphone themselves, one of their friends will.

After spending 6 months researching the effects of porn for a TV documentary, ex lad mag editor Martin Daubney, now a dad himself, looked back with regret at his involvement with the industry when he was interviewed about the programme:[36]

Internet porn [has] cast its dark shadow over the lives of millions of British teenagers. I used to be sceptical that porn was as damaging a force as the headlines … suggest. In the past I'd even defended pornography in university debates, on TV and on radio. I claimed it was our freedom of choice to watch it and said it could actually help add to adult relationships.

But what I saw during the making of the film changed my opinion of pornography forever.

The true stories of boys I met whose lives had been totally taken over by porn not only moved me to tears but also made

36 Martin Daubney, 'Experiment that convinced me online porn is the most pernicious threat facing children today', *Daily Mail*, September 2013. http://www.dailymail.co.uk/femail/article-2432591/Porn-pernicious-threat-facing-children-today-By-ex-lads-mag-editor-MARTIN-DAUBNEY.html.

*me incredibly angry that this is happening to our children. And
the looks of revulsion on those poor girl's faces in the playground
enraged me. I feel as if an entire generation's sexuality has been
hijacked by grotesque online porn.*

Talking with friends one day, the subject of children and porn came
up. Someone said that statistically speaking our boys had almost
certainly been looking at porn. Later, a friend who had been in the
group told me that she'd felt outraged and even slightly insulted –
that wouldn't happen in *her* family. But as she read more about the
culture our teens were growing up in, she had a nagging sense that
this might be right. She had no evidence – no laptop inadvertently
left open next to the maths homework or letters from the school. So
she ventured to ask them. She imagined that 'Have you ever seen
porn?' might be a naïve approach that would almost certainly be
met with a rebuff. Instead, one day in the car, she casually framed
the question, 'Just wondering … when did you first see porn?' She
wasn't sure what answer she was hoping for. While it wasn't, by then,
a surprise (and in case you are wondering, it was the first year at
secondary school at a friend's house), what did surprise her was the
nonchalant, matter of fact tone in which they answered. What she'd
thought was a big deal, her children seemed to take in their stride.

It seems she is not alone, and many of us parents have some
catching up to do. I recently met Lucy, a young single mum at a
Care for the Family parenting event. She was crying when she came
up to me at the end of the evening. She told me she had three lively
boys. Jake was the oldest, and until now he'd been a compliant child
who had caused her little concern. But last Friday at 7.30 a.m. all
that changed when a letter fell onto her doormat from the school.
As she read it, her heart missed a beat and her stomach churned; it
was from the Head asking her to come to a meeting after school the
next day. Some children had been accessing adult porn sites on their
smartphones, and it seemed that Jake was in the thick of it.

The news had sent Lucy spiralling into a state of anxiety.
Struggling against the tears, she told me that the initial shock was

followed by an overwhelming feeling of shame. What would other parents think? She felt guilty, alone, and didn't know where to begin to deal with the situation. As I listened to her story, my heart went out to her. I told her she wasn't the only parent to receive a letter like that from school, and she wasn't the only parent with a child whose combination of rising hormones and natural curiosity had led them to look at porn. Most of all, I reassured her that as a single mum it wasn't all her fault: the situation was part and parcel of parenting, whatever the shape of the family. The tears subsided and then she hugged me. I'd not given her clever answers or bright strategies, but I had been able to give her the awareness that she was not alone, and that knowledge had made all the difference to her.

At Care for the Family, we regularly have emails and calls from distraught parents who have made similar discoveries. They feel upset, guilty, and don't know where to go for help.

Kate was cooking the supper and asked Patrick, her husband, to pop upstairs to turn off the light in 9-year-old Joe's bedroom as it was well past his bedtime. At the bedroom door, Patrick could see Joe had made a den under the duvet, and it took him straight back to his own childhood. But when he crept into the room and pulled back the bedclothes to surprise his son, he got more than he bargained for. Young Joe was on his iPad looking at pictures of naked women. Kate was horrified, but Patrick was more philosophical. He remembered the magazines he used to look at in the 80s which he said didn't seem to have done him any harm.

While Joe's escapade may have been relatively harmless on that occasion, like many parents, Patrick hadn't grasped an important fact: the material available to our young people today – in both scale and content – is light years away from any magazines he may have looked at in his younger days.

Of course, there's nothing new about pornography, but what is different is that our children are the first generation to have access anywhere and anytime to unregulated free content. Internet-enabled smartphones and tablets mean they can now see porn at a speed and on a scale that previously wasn't possible, some of it portraying vicious and violent scenes that can leave an imprint on their lives forever. Like Patrick, many of us are blissfully ignorant of this and of the consequences.

I recently heard a heart-breaking interview with a young man called Matt. He first came across porn at a friend's house after school. Seeing a group of his friends gathered around a laptop, he walked over to find out what was causing such interest. He was amazed at what he saw. In the weeks that followed, he began looking at different porn sites in the privacy of his bedroom and was pleasantly surprised how much he enjoyed the sexual stimulation and release that it gave him. But what began as something he did once in a while began gradually to take a grip on his life and became a habit that he was unable to stop.

In order to satisfy his increasing appetite, he began looking at more explicit and brutal content. At college his porn habit continued … alongside a series of failed relationships with girls. Shortly after college he married, but as a couple they had problems in their sexual relationship. He believed his inability to maintain an erection was a physical problem and went to his GP. The medication he was prescribed only made things worse. He then went to see a counsellor who suggested that he watch porn with his wife to try to overcome his issues – advice they didn't follow. Matt explained what happened after that:

> I was desperate. Eventually I was referred to a therapist who diagnosed 'porn-induced ED (erectile dysfunction)'. I couldn't believe what she was saying. She explained that over the years, watching porn had conditioned my brain to be aroused only by seeing sexual images on screens, and it had left me unable to be aroused by my wife. At the time, with all my friends watching porn it seemed a simple pleasure and I didn't think there was anything wrong with it. It's only now that I understand the damage it causes. Porn kills intimacy. Young people need to know about this and not have to go through what I have been through.

Matt has now received the help and support he needed, but his story is not unique. In a recent interview,[37] Angela Gregory, a psychosexual therapist at Nottingham University Hospital, commented that over the last 10 years, she has seen an increasing number of young men presenting with sexual difficulties that have their root in porn and chat room use. Many young people, girls as well as boys, are growing up casually watching porn in the same way they would watch a romcom or sport on TV. They consider it a 'normal' pastime, not realising the chemical changes it brings about in the brain, its addictive effect, and the fact that it can ruin their ability to build a healthy sexual relationship.

As a society, we can no longer bury our heads in the sand. Fifty years ago, smoking was an accepted social practice. Unbelievably, advertisements featured doctors promoting cigarettes and pregnant mothers celebrating smoking in pregnancy because it gave the 'win-win' of smaller babies and easy labour. Yet today, cigarettes are locked away in grey cabinets behind the counter, packets come with government health warnings, and smoking is banned in public places because society has realised the damage it causes and has taken action. In the same way, we have been ignorant of the damage that watching pornography can do to our health, especially the health of our children, and again it is time to take action.

As parents, many of us need a wake-up call to understand the seriousness of the issue. If you are still in doubt, here are three reasons why this matters:

Porn is addictive

Even if science wasn't your favourite subject at school, it's important to take a moment to understand the effect on the human brain of watching too much porn. We know that pleasurable activity (including watching porn) causes dopamine, the chemical responsible for reward and pleasure, to be released. So the more

---

37 Simon Mundie, 'Easy access to online porn is "damaging" men's health, says NHS therapist', *BBC Newsbeat*, 15 August 2016. http://www.bbc.co.uk/newsbeat/article/37058019/easy-access-to-online-porn-is-damaging-mens-health-says-nhs-therapist.

porn that is watched, the more dopamine is released in this 'reward centre' of the brain.

But here lies the problem. Repeated dopamine surges mean that the brain becomes desensitised to its effects, so after time, a bigger dopamine hit is needed to produce the same feeling. In the same way that, over time, drug users need more drugs to experience a high, so those using porn need more and more stimulation to achieve the same effect.

Dr Jeffery Satinover, a psychiatrist, psychoanalyst, physicist and former fellow in Psychiatry at Yale University, graphically described the addictive effect of pornography to the US Congress:

> It is as though we have devised a form of heroin 100 times more powerful than before, usable in the privacy of one's own home and injected directly to the brain through the eyes.[38]

Scientists know that watching too much porn can actually rewire the brain. The human brain has an incredible ability to reorganise itself by forming new connections between brain cells as it adapts to new experiences. This ability to change is known as the brain's 'plasticity'. If you become an expert in something new, the area in your brain that deals with this type of skill will actually grow. A study involving London taxi drivers is an interesting example of this as it has shown that they have a larger hippocampus than London bus drivers.[39] This is the part of the brain used for navigation and spatial awareness (which anyone travelling with me can attest is sadly lacking in my case). Bus drivers follow a limited set of defined routes, whereas taxi drivers have to navigate to different destinations from different starting points, and their brains have adapted accordingly.

Over a lifetime, our brains continue to reorganise themselves according to our experiences, and watching porn is no exception. Each time someone looks at porn, dopamine consolidates the new connections made.[40] It is as if a small footpath through a meadow

38 Morgan Bennett, 'The New Narcotic', *Public Discourse*, October 2013. http://www.thepublicdiscourse. com/2013/10/10846.
39 E. A. Maguire, et al, 'London Taxi Drivers and Bus Drivers: A Structural MRI and Neuropsychological Analysis', *Hippocampus*, 2006, vol. 16, pp. 1091–1101.
40 Gary Wilson, *Your Brain on Porn: Internet Pornography and the Emerging Science of Addiction*, Commonwealth Publishing, 2015.

becomes a well-trodden path; the more often it is walked, the more established it becomes, eventually becoming a wide and busy highway. For young people, the effect is even more significant because their brains are more malleable; as we have seen, the prefrontal cortex of the teenage brain is still developing, so making them even more vulnerable.

If this sounds all gloom and doom, there *is* hope! It follows that if the brain is always changing, although it may be difficult, it's never too late to change the pathways by forming new habits. But better still to not get involved in the first place.

Porn gives unrealistic expectations of real relationships

Porn bombards our young people with images that set wildly unrealistic expectations for real-life relationships. And it starts so young. Most of us will, I imagine, be shocked by one parent's account of her primary school child asking, 'Why do you have to wear masks when you have sex?'[41]

The fundamental problem with porn is that it gives our children the message that sex is a performance which is divorced from relationship, from consent, from respect, from faithfulness, and from commitment.

Hard-core videos portray something that has nothing to do with the loving and intimate act of sexual intercourse. Kissing, hugging and tenderness are absent and there is an emphasis on oral sex. Women have surgically enlarged breasts, men have penis enlargements, pubic hair is non-existent, and girls who don't go along with the trend for porn-inspired waxing are considered 'ugly' and 'gross'.

The images of tiny waists and Kardashian bums put an incredible pressure on girls to act and look a particular way (well-nigh impossible for even the most shapely among us). Sixteen-year-old Marna said, 'The pressure on us is massive. I know I can't compete,

---

41 Suzie Hayman and John Coleman, *Parents and Digital Technology*, Routledge, 2016, p. 59.

but it doesn't stop me feeling that I have to.' These images also do our boys no favours by giving them unrealistic expectations of women and sex. And it's not just confined to what they see, but what they hear; some of the language used is brutal. As author Allison Havey put it:

> It's not only the images. The language on pornographic sites is very particular too: verbs such as 'nailed', 'hammered', 'screwed', 'pummelled'. Anyone would think it was an advert for a DIY store.[42]

You may or may not be surprised to hear that many teens believe that the best way to learn about sex is to view porn. Author Peggy Orenstein writes:

> Kids look at porn, in part, as an instruction manual, even though it's about as realistic as pro wrestling ... Girls would ask me all the time, 'My boyfriend wants to know why I don't make all those noises like porn stars during sex,' and I would say, 'Because [porn] is a movie.'[43]

But real life is not a movie. And here is the irony. A healthy sexual relationship is the culmination of the closest, most loving, tender and intimate connection possible between two real people. But porn has exploited sex in such a way that it has become an impersonal solitary act of masturbation while watching fantasy images. Our teenagers have been sold a counterfeit – and many have no idea.

Porn is becoming 'normal'

Porn is everywhere. In fact, *The Bailey Review* in 2011 described the sexualised culture of today as 'the "wallpaper" of children's lives'.[44] A head teacher who tried to do something about porn in her school

42 Joanna Moorhead, 'How porn is damaging our children's future sex lives', *The Guardian*, 10 September 2016.
43 Peggy Orenstein, *Girls and Sex: Navigating the Complicated New Landscape*, Harper, March 2016.
44 Reg Bailey, 'Letting Children Be Children. Report of an Independent Review of the Commercialisation and Sexualisation of Childhood', Department of Education, 2011.

was told by parents as well as pupils that she was old-fashioned and that 'everyone does it'.[45] And an American study found that 56% of young people considered it wrong to not recycle (which, of course, is a good thing), but only 32% of the same children thought viewing porn was wrong.[46]

If you like stats, here are some sobering ones to think about:

- The single largest consumer of porn is 12- to 17-year-old-boys.[47]
- Of 3,000 boys aged 13–18, 81% said they looked at porn.[48]
- An NSPCC survey of 1000 children revealed that over 50% of 11-year-olds had seen porn online and almost all (94%) have seen it by the age of 14.[49]
- Children were as likely to stumble across pornography (28%) as to search for it deliberately (19%).[50]
- Substantial minorities of older children (42% of 12–16-year-olds) wanted to try things out they had seen in pornography.[51]

Even if our young people don't actively look for porn, it may well find them. (I recently heard of a mum whose son was recently doing a project on the City of London and got more than he bargained for after innocently typing 'Big Ben' in the search engine.) Remembering the day she discovered her daughter had been secretly watching hard-core pornographic videos with friends, after being introduced to the videos by another child, is still upsetting for another mum:

She's 8. She still believes in Santa Claus and the Tooth Fairy. You think you are doing everything right and then you discover

45 Barbara McMahone, 'Teenage girls and sex: do you really know what's going on?', *The Times*, 28 May 2016.
46 David Kinnaman, 'The Porn Phenomenon: The Impact of Pornography in the Digital Age', *Barna Group*, April 2016.
47 'The Porn Standard: Children, Pornography on the Internet', *Third Way*, July 2005. http://content.thirdway.org/publications/14/Third_Way_Report_-_The_Porn_Standard_-_Children_and_Pornography_on_the_Internet.pdf.
48 'How porn is damaging our children's future sex lives', *The Guardian*, 10 September 2016.
49 E. Martellozzo, et al, '"I wasn't sure it was normal to watch it …": A quantitative and qualitative examination of the impact of online pornography on the values, attitudes, beliefs, and behaviours of children and young people.' NSPCC/OCC, 2016.
50 *Ibid*.
51 *Ibid*.

you've been invaded by an intrusive, outside, evil scummy force. It's so gut-wrenching. The sadness of an innocence lost. You only get one childhood.[52]

The average age of first exposure to porn is 11 years old, when children often come across it while doing their homework.[53]

Many mainstream music videos watched by children (check out Britney Spears, Miley Cyrus, or Rihanna just for starters) are, arguably, inches from porn. This indirect messaging has the effect of making porn or near-porn a 'normal' part of life for our children.

All this is not intended to be alarmist or to engender a sense of panic, but to open our eyes to the issues and, in doing so, equip us to protect our children from the dangers of porn and prevent them becoming its victims. Let's not walk blindly into a society where 'porn is the norm' for our children.

WHAT PARENTS CAN DO

✓ Talk about it

At home, we can set up every possible external protection there is, but the same filters may not be in place on public Wi-Fi. And of course, there may well be no controls at all at a friend's house or on a friend's device. So as well as using filters and controls in our homes, we must also equip our children to operate their own controls – to self-regulate. This means that we need to be talking to them positively about sex, about relationships, about faithfulness and, in this context, the issue of porn. There is no room for us to feel embarrassed about this or even worried that if we talk about porn it will fuel their curiosity. All children are sexual beings and are going to be curious about sex ... so it's a lot better to instil values in our children before the porn industry gets to them.

---

52 Sara Israelsen-Hartley, 'How to talk to your kind about porn', *Deseret News*, 14 August 2014. http://www.deseretnews.com/article/865608715/Innocence-interrupted-How-to-eliminate-shame-increase-education-when-kids-stumble-onto-porn.html.
53 'The Porn Standard: Children, Pornography on the Internet', *Third Way*, July 2005. http://content.thirdway.org/publications/14/Third_Way_Report_-_The_Porn_Standard_-_Children_and_Pornography_on_the_Internet.pdf.

'You look very uncomfortable, Dad.
Is this about sex, porn or drugs?'

A report commissioned by the NSPCC and the Children's Commissioner last year found that teenagers wanted to find out about sex and relationships in ways that were 'safe, private and credible'[54] and Ed Brook, who works with the national sexual health service for under-25s, said in an interview with *The Times* that 'Year 10 school surveys "overwhelmingly" reveal that teens want mum or dad, more than peers or teachers, to talk about sex. They want to hear it from their parents.'[55] Who better fits the bill? As their parents, we are the most significant influence in their lives ... and yet 75% of parents avoid discussing porn with their teens.[56]

Cindy Gallop, an Oxford graduate who founded the website *www.makelovenotporn.com* said, 'We're at a zeitgeist moment. You cannot avoid your children seeing porn. If parents want their child to be happy they have to tackle it.'[57]

As their children had grown up, Tim and Jade had talked to them about the facts of life but had never mentioned porn. They knew it was an issue they needed to address at some point, but it felt awkward and alien territory, and they had no idea how to begin. They agreed that Tim would talk to the boys and Jade to the girls. Tim put it off for ages, and then one day at work he read an article about the effect of porn on children and realised he couldn't procrastinate any longer. Sitting round the kitchen table that evening, he awkwardly blurted out that he'd read an article that he wanted to talk to them about. He admitted that he was clumsy and slightly embarrassed and didn't make a great job of it, but said that it probably wasn't as bad as he'd feared. He realised that his children knew more than he did, and in hindsight his main regret was that he hadn't done it 5 years earlier.

And in these discussions, we have to do better than just saying, 'Don't watch porn.' Talking to our children about sex can feel embarrassing, but embarrassment is a luxury we can't afford. If *we* don't talk to them, they may well get unhelpful information about sex from friends or, worse still, from viewing porn.

54 E. Martellozzo, et al, "'I wasn't sure it was normal to watch it ...": A quantitative and qualitative examination of the impact of online pornography on the values, attitudes, beliefs, and behaviours of children and young people.' NSPCC/OCC, 2016.
55 Barbara McMahon, 'Teenage girls and sex: do you really know what's going on?', *The Times*, 28 May 2016.
56 Allison Havey and Deana Puccio, *Sex, Likes and Social Media*, Vermilion, 2016, p. 95, quoted in *Psychologies*.
57 Barbara McMahon, 'Teenage girls and sex: do you really know what's going on?', *The Times*, 28 May 2016.

We found over the years that our children generally didn't respond well to the 'big talk' or lecture; it usually resulted in embarrassment on both sides and a sigh of relief once it was over. Better was the 'little and often' approach; fostering a continuing open and honest conversation, planting seeds, perhaps commenting on the values behind adverts, articles or programmes, listening to their point of view, and explaining to them that porn is as far removed from the reality of real sex as films are to real life.

And we can start when they are young. When toddlers ask where the baby guinea pig came from we can begin a conversation in preparation for the more challenging questions that will no doubt follow hard on its heels! At our Care for the Family events we often say to parents, 'When it comes to your *own* children, nobody knows your child like you and nobody loves your child like you. Have confidence in your parenting.' In the same way, as parents we must have confidence in talking to our children about sex and relationships – there is nobody better placed than us. Schools can do a great job teaching about sex, but they only convey the facts. As parents, we can talk to our children about sex in the context of relationships and our values, remembering to keep it simple, age-appropriate, and positive. Above all, let them know they can always talk to us if they see anything that frightens, confuses or upsets them, and that they won't be in trouble.

There are some useful resources we can use to help our children which are listed in the appendix. For younger children the NSPCC's friendly singing and dancing pants-wearing dinosaur, Pantosaurus, helps start simple conversations. This includes teaching children the acronym PANTS: **P**rivates are private; **A**lways remember your body belongs to you; **N**o means no; **T**alk about secrets that upset you; **S**peak up, someone can help.

And the Naked Truth Project suggests teaching children the 3 Ts: **T**urn away; **T**urn it off; and **T**ell a trusted adult. It also suggests telling them that 'talking about it is always best, no matter how bad it seems'.

For older teenagers a YouTube animation uploaded by Thames Valley Police brilliantly uses different scenarios of people offering each other a cup of tea to address the issue of consenting sex.[58] One mum recently told me she had watched the clip with her daughter and that it had resulted in a great conversation about sex, faithfulness and marriage, and had empowered her daughter to have the confidence to say 'no'.

WHEN THINGS GO WRONG

If you discover that your child has been accessing porn or that porn is an issue for them, it's important to be there for them and point them in the direction of any help they need. Showing our child unconditional love and acceptance (see Chapter 7) at a time like this may be very hard for many parents. We first have to cope with our own emotions, perhaps anger as well as dismay, hurt, and feeling at a loss to understand how this has come about. But compassionate love and understanding for our child is vital to dealing well with this issue. Realise that they are likely to be suffering from extreme shame and embarrassment, so help them feel safe enough to be open with you about the full story.

While there is no room for complacency, don't let the prospect of porn and the digital age overwhelm you: 50% of 11-year-olds may have looked at porn, but that means 50% haven't. And of those that do, it certainly doesn't mean they will become addicted. Putting the safeguards in place, beginning open and honest conversations from early childhood and, most importantly, giving them real-life positive examples of healthy relationships will put them in the best possible place for withstanding the pressures of growing up in a sexualised society and digital age.

58 Thames Valley Police, 'Tea and Consent'. https://www.youtube.com/watch?v=pZwvrxVavnQ.

CHAPTER 9

SEXTING

I was educated at an all-girls school, and I still remember the excitement one day in assembly when it was announced that we would be putting on a play in partnership with the local boys' school. Never before had so many girls wanted a career on the stage. Hoping for the lead role (Joan of Arc) I went along to the auditions and ended up being cast as the executioner. (To this day I still don't know why that role wasn't given to a boy!) It was at the first rehearsal that I met Ian, and when it finished he passed me a note asking if we could meet up. I was flattered and excited, and I returned the favour. And so our (shortlived!) relationship began. Flirting, dating, and taking a romantic interest in peers is all part of growing up, but instead of scruffy notes passed hastily during art lessons, the process will be conducted by text or online messages. And, for our teenagers today, this can involve photos and images, often of a sexual nature.

Sexting is when someone sends sexually explicit texts or photos or videos of themselves or others naked or semi naked using a mobile or other device. Many young people see this as flirting; some even view it as a necessary precursor to starting a relationship. Sending a revealing selfie can make someone feel good about themselves and may be seen as harmless fun. Boys may ask for a picture of a girl in a skimpy top, topless, or even naked to see if they pass muster before asking them out on a date. And many girls, not wanting to offend, feel under immense pressure to agree. One 15-year-old said, 'My boyfriend asked for a topless selfie and I thought that if I didn't send it he wouldn't like me.' And it's not just girls; boys also may feel under pressure to send pictures of themselves – in a macho pose, topless to show off a six-pack gym body, or even naked.

In an article on the issue, *The Times* reported:

Britain is suffering from a sexting crisis with tens of thousands of school-children caught sharing sexual imagery online in the

*past three years ... Data from 50 of Britain's biggest secondary
schools showed that more than a third of all sexting cases
involved children aged 12 and 13.*[59]

Commenting on the data, an NSPCC spokesman said that the
situation was particularly worrying because in one in ten cases these
pictures were sent to adults: 'Sexting can make young people targets
for sex offenders or set them up for bullying by their peers.'[60]

'The Wireless Report', a survey of 1,000 young people in 2014,[61]
revealed that:

- 37% of 13- to 25-year-olds have sent a naked photo of
themselves via a smartphone app.
- 49% believe sexting is harmless fun.
- Girls were twice as likely to send a naked photo of
themselves more than once a week than boys.
- 24% have had a naked photo shared without their consent.

We have already seen that in adolescence the prefrontal cortex
of the brain, which plays an important part in problem-solving
and impulse control, isn't fully formed. This means that risks and
consequences are not properly weighed up – the brakes are not yet
in place – and, of course, this can come at a cost. What may start
off as a private message can be shared (and even manipulated) by
others in a matter of seconds. According to one child protection
expert, nearly half of all schoolgirls have regretted sending images
via Instagram and Snapchat, and the NSPCC has reported that
Childline counselling sessions about sexting are on the increase.[62]

Sharing sexually explicit material without consent in order to
cause embarrassment and harm ('revenge porn') is another issue
we should be aware of as parents. Leo and Chloe are both 16. They
began dating and sent romantic texts to each other which gradually

59 Alexi Mostrous, Elizabeth Rigby, 'Schools hit by sexting epidemic', *The Times*, 12 March 2016.
60 *Ibid.*
61 Ditch the Label, 'The Wireless Report (2014): How young people between the ages of 13–25 engage with smartphone technology and naked photos'. https://www.ditchthelabel.org/wp-content/uploads/2016/07/wireless2014.pdf.
62 H. Bentley, et al, 'How Safe Are Our Children? The most comprehensive overview of child protection in the UK',
NSPCC, 2016.

SEXTING

became more sexual in nature. This was followed by photos and then videos. At a party one evening, Leo saw Chloe with another boy and to get his own back he decided to post a nude picture of her on Facebook. Before she was aware of what had happened, the image had been shared among all their friends. Chloe, ashamed and embarrassed, was devastated. The picture was taken down fairly quickly, but the damage had already been done. (Since 2015 a law against revenge porn has made it illegal to disclose a private sexual photograph or film without the consent of the person depicted in the content and with the intent to cause them distress.)

A friend's son recently had a very sobering experience. He began a conversation online with someone he didn't know, but believed to be a girl his own age. Over the weeks that followed she encouraged him to send increasingly sexually explicit images to her, and then one day he received a blackmail threat: if he didn't send money she would post the images on Facebook. This lad went into an utter panic. He shut down the account and after a few anxious and sleepless nights told his mother who was able to offer him support and advice. Fortunately for him, the threats were not carried out, but it could so easily have resulted in actions that would have scarred him and his reputation for life.

A couple of things to bear in mind about sexting:

It's illegal for under-18s
Many parents (and children!) may be surprised to know that it is illegal in the UK to take, hold or share indecent pictures of anyone under 18. So even though the legal age of consent for sexual intercourse is 16, the legal age to send a sexually explicit photo is 18.[63] If under-18s take a nude photo and share it (even with friends of the same age) they are breaking the law. (Whether the police take action is another matter, but the law is there for their protection.)

What goes online, stays online
Once you've hit 'send', you have lost control of that picture. While apps such as Snapchat promise to automatically delete your 'snap' after 10 seconds, this can't be relied upon as a means of ensuring it

63 Sexual Offences Act, 2003.

89

is still under your control. The recipient could take a screen shot and then pass it on, and there are many other ways in which the photo can be shared and misused by others. There really is no 'delete' button.

WHAT PARENTS CAN DO

✓ Talk about it

The results of a YouGov poll last year asking parents what issues affecting their children they were concerned about, showed that more were worried about sexting than they were about smoking or drinking.[64] Despite this concern, however, the NSPCC comments that most parents have a 'worrying level of ignorance' about the issue.[65]

Along with so many other areas, a key strategy for us as parents is to have conversations as early as possible with our children, not waiting until it happens. In the same way as we need to talk to them about porn, we can talk to our children about sexting, healthy relationships, and why they might want to send the picture in the first place.

Childline's *Zipit*[66] is a great app that helps children 'get flirty chat back on the right track' with tips on how to keep control, and clever comebacks to download and send if they are asked to send a naked photo. There are lots to choose from including a picture of a tortoise with the caption, 'Slow Down', a supermarket trolley and the caption, 'Don't push too far', and even a ram with the caption, 'Horny? Not my problem'. And a good video to watch with them is *Exposed* by the Child Exploitation and Online Protection Centre which shows what can potentially happen as a result of sharing images. See appendix for more information.

---

64 PHSE Association, 'Parents call for education to address sexting by children and young people', July 2016. https://www.pshe-association.org.uk/news/parents-call-education-address-sexting-children.

65 Sian Griffiths, 'Parents too shy to tackle sexting', *The Times*, 14 August 2016.

66 Childline, *Zipit*. https://www.childline.org.uk/info-advice/bullying-abuse-safety/online-mobile-safety/sexting/zipit-app.

✓ Encourage your children to 'think twice'

Help them weigh up the consequences carefully, and encourage them to *think, think,* and then *think* again before they post something. When the government is drafting legislation on matters of national security, it often includes what is known as a 'double lock' – checks and balances to go through before action can be taken. Encourage your teens to have a 'double lock' in place – a mental checklist of things to consider before they post a photo and particularly before sharing another person's image. Ask them open questions to help them reflect: How will it stay private? How can you stop it being passed on? If it was passed on, who might see it? How would that make you feel? How would that make them feel? A good test is to ask, 'Would you do this offline? Would you really stand topless in front of your geography class or ask your friend to stand naked outside McDonalds?' Remind them that doing these things online is no different.

WHEN THINGS GO WRONG

A couple I met with recently told me how their daughter had come to them in great distress. She had sent a topless selfie to her boyfriend, which had subsequently been uploaded to Facebook without any privacy controls. The photo had spread like wildfire – all her friends and classmates had seen it. Their daughter was humiliated and inconsolable. She couldn't face her friends and didn't want to go to school. Her mum and dad had no idea what to do. They were good, loving parents who were completely wrong-footed by what had happened and were struggling to manage their own feelings of anger and shame, while knowing they needed to be there for their daughter. We chatted through the situation, and a few weeks later I received an email from them:

Thank you so much for listening. We just needed somewhere to 'vent' as we knew being mad with her wouldn't help anyone. The school have been brilliant, and we have managed to get the photos taken down. It's been such a lesson for all of us.

If you find your child has sent a selfie that they regret, stay calm (sometimes easier said than done), reassure them and help them deal with the consequences. They may be worried and embarrassed, so reassure them that we all make mistakes and that, as hard as it may be, you will help them see the situation through. Try to find out as much about the context as possible, in particular why they sent it, and ask them who the photo has been sent to and where it has been shared.

Help them to delete the photo or photos from their phone and online accounts, but keep copies of the evidence in case you need it. If possible, see if they can contact the person the image was sent to and ask them to delete it as well.

When sexting messages are shared on social media or other sites you can report it with your child and ask the service providers or website to take the image down. Inform your child's school about what has happened and ask for their help both in controlling the circulation and supporting your child. If the image has been shared by one of their pupils, the school can help you approach them directly. If it is more serious and you think your child has been coerced into sending an image, or if it has been shared with an adult, you may need to get in contact with the police. See appendix for more information.

A Pew Research Center report seems to have summed up the current situation well:

> *The desire for risk-taking and sexual exploration during the teenage years, combined with a constant connection via mobile devices, creates a 'perfect storm' for sexting. [Teenagers'] coming-of-age mistakes and transgressions have never been so easily transmitted and archived for others to see.*[67]

It's time to take action before the storm heads our family's way – and as parents we are in the very best place to do this.

67 Amanda Lenhart, et al., 'Teens and Mobile Phones: Text messaging explodes as teens embrace it as the centerpiece of their communication strategies with friends', *Pew Research Center*, 20 April 2010.

CHAPTER 10

ONLINE BULLYING

'Night, love! Sleep tight. Don't let the bedbugs bite.' Crystal paused on the stairs. Her mum said the same thing every night. It got on her nerves a bit – though she admitted to herself that she'd probably miss it if Mum suddenly *didn't* say it. It was 10.30 p.m. and her heart was hammering. As she opened her bedroom door, she felt sick. She undressed slowly and climbed under the duvet. Her comfy mattress felt like stone. The minutes ticked by and she stiffened – waiting. Perhaps tonight would be different ...

But then it came: the familiar beep from the depths of her school bag. She'd left her phone there deliberately, rather than putting it on her bedside table, a visible threat. She screwed her eyes tight and desperately tried to sleep, but after some minutes the beep came again. It was impossible to ignore. She crawled out of bed, her stomach cramping. Unearthing her phone from her bag, she clicked onto the message. It was, of course, from one of her tormentors. Since escaping them at the end of school, she'd seen the Facebook comments, but in the last couple of hours there had been silence. She'd known it would be short-lived. Her phone beeped again. She read the text and stuffed the phone under her pillow. She waited, her eyes open in the dark.

For children today there is no escape from the school bully at the end of the day. They are there on the bus and during the walk home; they lurk as homework is done and the evening meal is eaten; they force their way into the bedroom at night. There is no safe haven. The bully can reach their prey at anytime and anywhere.

The scale and the speed of digital communication also means

that what starts off as an unkind joke or two can quickly spiral out of control into abuse. Comments about weight, body shape, clothes, glasses, hair colour, skin, lack of sporting ability or any other number of issues are all there to be viewed by and passed on to others further and further afield.

The other day my friend told me about her 13-year-old niece, Emma. Emma seems to have hit puberty a little bit ahead of her peers and is already suffering with some unwelcome teenage spots. Apparently, her 'friends' went on Facebook, clicked on her profile photo, counted up the number of spots and then 'shared' the photo with the spots highlighted. What does that kind of experience do for a child's self-esteem?

And unkind messaging isn't limited to teenagers. The *Today* programme on Radio 4 recently discussed online safety and featured an interview with Matteo who is in year 5.[68] Matteo plays a game online where one person has to draw something while the other person guesses what it is. 'They couldn't guess what I drew, and then someone called me an a-hole. I felt really upset so I told my mum straight away,' he told Victoria Derbyshire. Matteo's mum said she blocked that person but could do 'absolutely nothing' about it. 'I feel extremely guilty that he had access to that.'

While some children will take the odd joke or insult in their stride, if bullying is repeated and abusive it can have a devastating effect on their mental health. Schoolwork can suffer, and some may resort to coping mechanisms which lead to self-harming, eating disorders, drug or alcohol abuse.[69]

Online bullying is when the perpetrator uses social media and messages on the internet to bully another person, usually repeatedly. Matters are made worse still because abusive and humiliating messages and images can be shared, which means that they are seen by more people and for a longer period than any other kinds of bullying. And it's more common than many of us would think. Almost one in five young people in the UK have been affected by online bullying, according to research commissioned by the

68 'Online Safety: Internet "not designed for children"', *BBC News*, 5 January 2017. http://www.bbc.co.uk/news/education-38508888.
69 Dr Hayley van Zwanenberg, quoted in 'Analysis: Impulsive act that can easily ruin a young life', *The Times*, 12 March 2016.

National Children's Bureau.[70] And in a survey of 1,024 UK 11- to 16-year-olds about their experience on social networking sites, it was found that 37% reported that they had been upset by trolling in the last year.[71]

Online bullying can be carried out in a number of ways. These include:

- Sending hurtful, nasty texts and emails.
- Posting someone's personal information or images without their permission.
- Putting a humiliating video of someone on sites such as YouTube, including 'happy slapping' – videos of personal attacks.
- Setting up profiles that make fun of someone on social media such as Facebook.
- Deliberately sending someone viruses to damage their computer.
- Making abusive comments about another player on a gaming site.

The most common impact on children of online bullying is on their confidence, self-esteem and mental and emotional well-being. Most young people think it's as harmful as other forms of bullying and some consider it worse because the abuse is 'permanent' in the form of an online record which can be shared with many people very quickly and cannot be deleted.[72]

Common responses from those who are being bullied are loss of appetite, poor sleep, anxiety, withdrawal, missing school and stopping socialising. Cyberbullying has also been found to have a

---

70 N. O'Brian, et al, 'The Impact of Cyberbullying on Young People's Mental Health', Anglia Ruskin University/ National Children's Bureau, 2010.

71 C. Lilley, et al, 'Experiences of 11–16 year olds on social networking sites: a survey of young people's online experiences and coping strategies', NSPCC, 2014. https://www.nspcc.org.uk/services-and-resources/research-and-resources/2014/experiences-of-11-16-year-olds-on-social-networking-sites.

72 Vodafone survey on teen cyberbullying conducted by YouGov, 2015. https://mediacentre.vodafone.co.uk/press-release/groundbreaking-vodafone-global-survey-reveals-43-of-teens-think-cyberbullying-a-bigger-problem-than-drug-abuse.

particular link to depression in teenagers.[73] Sadly there have been some high-profile cases of victims of bullying being driven to suicide. After years of relentless bullying in school and on social media, 17-year-old Felix Alexander took his own life in April 2016. His mother Lucy said that the bullying had begun with unkindness and social isolation and then, with the advent of social media, over the years it had become cruel and overwhelming.[74]

WHAT PARENTS CAN DO

✓ Watch out for signs that your child may be experiencing online bullying:

- A sudden change in the amount of time they are on their phone or computer – either more or less – might signal a possible problem. (But remember that a child's interest will ebb and flow, so it will all depend on the context.)
- Suddenly having lots of new contacts on their social media account – they may not all be 'friends'.
- Changes in their mood when they are on social media. Watch out for how they seem when they put their phone away or close their laptop, particularly if they are nervous or jumpy.
- Asking you how they can block others on, or delete, their social media account (or finding out that they have done this).
- Eating and sleeping problems, or unexplained physical symptoms such as headaches or stomach upsets.
- Negative statements about themselves, others or life in general and any indications of a dip in self-esteem, for example, head held low.

73 'Is social media bad for young people's health', *The Guardian*, 20 January, 2017. https://www.theguardian.com/mental-health-research-matters/2017/jan/20/is-social-media-bad-for-young-peoples-mental-health.
74 Nicola Slawson, 'Mother of teenager who killed himself appeals for kindness online', *The Guardian*, 5 October 2016. https://www.theguardian.com/society/2016/oct/05/felix-alexander-mother-lucy-open-letter-worcester.

Do remember that the last two warning signs may be indications of problems with completely different causes, so these alone do not mean that your child is being cyberbullied.

✓ Give your child your support

When our daughter was having a particularly difficult time with a friendship group at school, and unkind texts and Facebook posts were flying about, my advice to her was, 'Just ignore it'. She has since told me how unhelpful that recommendation was (0/10 there for my parenting skills!) Rather too late in the day, my daughter (now 20-something) tells me a much better approach would have been to have listened to her (instead of jumping in with my timely advice) and reassured her that the bullying wasn't her fault. It can be really upsetting as a parent to hear about, but do your best to remain calm and let your child know that you will help them through it.

✓ Don't stop your child going online

If children are the butt of unkind jokes or the victim of bullying, it will be almost impossible for them to 'just ignore it', and telling them not to go online or stopping them using their devices is also likely to be counterproductive. We might as well be asking them not to breathe, and it would most probably lead to them feeling more isolated and cut off from any network of friends that they do have.

✓ Tell your child not to reply

All bullies are looking for a reaction, so advise your child not to reply or retaliate in any way. If an online conversation becomes abusive or makes them feel uncomfortable, they should simply leave it.

✓ Block messages

Tell your child to block the sender and report them to their social media network or the gaming platform.

✓ Get outside support

Talk to your friends to get support for yourself, and, if necessary, go to your child's school as they should have an anti-bullying policy. In extreme cases, and especially if you feel your child is in danger, consider informing the police. Think also about whether to get outside help for your child. Counselling may be of benefit both during and after the episode.

When *our* child is the bully

As unwelcome as the thought is, as parents we may have to face up to the fact that our child is joining in with bullies by acquiescing in an unkind campaign or even that they are the main perpetrator. As parents, it's easy to be defensive about our children, but it's important to find out the full story. If our child *is* bullying online, we won't be helping them (or their victim) by denying it. If this happens, it's important to remember that we all say things we don't mean at times, and rather than jumping in too hastily, we need to try to discover what is really going on.

There are a number of different motives for online bullying, sometimes it's done out of anger, frustration or to get revenge; sometimes it is done simply out of boredom and for entertainment – to get laughs or a reaction. Some children do it to make themselves feel more powerful, tormenting others to boost their ego. And then there are those who think they are righting wrongs – perhaps standing up for someone else or taking a stand against an issue they see as unjust. Finally, there are those who have simply bullied almost by accident – not thinking through what they are doing or not realising the impact it will have. One of the deterrents to face-to-face bullying is that the perpetrator is made aware that the recipient is a real person with real feelings. With online bullying the contact is less personal because it is all done via a screen and may be even harder to combat.

WHAT PARENTS CAN DO

✓ Talk it through

As upset as we might feel, it's important to stay calm and talk things through. In the same way as if they were involved in sexting, ask your children open questions and try to help them understand the effect of their actions on the other person's feelings. Without face-to-face connection, it can be easy for comments to be misinterpreted or misunderstood, so emphasise the importance of thinking through what they post online. Something that initially seems funny, might easily end up causing great harm.

See *www.stopcyberbullying.org* for some great age-linked questions children can go through with you or by themselves (see appendix).

✓ Don't condone it

There may be factors that help to explain your child's behaviour, but while taking these into account, it's important not to blame someone else. Show your child that taking responsibility for their own actions is the right thing to do. If they were bullying online in retaliation to being bullied themselves (or on another child's behalf), tell them that two wrongs don't make a right and will just encourage the bully's behaviour.

If appropriate, help them face up to their actions and, as hard as it may be to do, apologise to the person concerned.

✓ Don't confiscate their devices

You may want to limit their online access, but this could make the situation worse and encourage them to find other ways to get online.

✓ Try to find out the reasons

Remember that the old saying 'hurting people hurt people' has a lot of truth in it, so take time to see if there is anything going on in your child's life that has made them act in this way. Think about any areas in your child's life that may be upsetting or angering them and leading them to express these feelings online.

CHAPTER 11

GROOMING

Kayleigh was 15 when she received a friend request on Facebook from another girl:

> *She was very friendly – we began chatting and we found we had lots in common. After a few weeks, she asked me to send her a topless photo of myself. I didn't reply, but she kept on asking. I was really worried and didn't know what to do, but ended up telling my mum. The police eventually got involved. They contacted Facebook and discovered that the message had in fact come from a man who was older than my dad.*

It seems that every day there is another story about online grooming. It's an issue to strike terror into the heart of any parent, and while the purpose of this book is not to scaremonger, sadly it is something that we cannot ignore. The groomer's method is all about befriending and building an emotional relationship with a child, gaining their trust in order to take advantage of them sexually. The Child Exploitation and Online Protection Centre reports that 13- and 14-year-olds represent the largest single victim group.[75] This may include the groomer having sexual conversations with them online or by text message, getting them to send images or videos of themselves naked, doing something sexually explicit on webcam or meeting up with them in person. Grooming also takes place face-to-face of course, but the anonymity of digital communication means there is huge scope for the predator.

Groomers may not always be strangers; in some cases they may have met the children socially and use the internet to build a relationship with them. They may be male or female, old or young and generally use a false identity with fake profile pictures, building

75 Children's Society, 'What is child sexual exploitation?'. http://www.childrenssociety.org.uk/what-is-child-sexual-exploitation?

the relationship gradually by pretending to share mutual interests and experiences. Often they join social networks used by young people and pretend to be one of them. Once a rapport and trust is established, they will bring sexual experiences into the online conversation, ask them to send sexual photographs and even try to meet the child.

Grooming can also take place via computer gaming. Breck Bednar was a 14-year-old boy who loved technology and online gaming. He was groomed and manipulated by someone he played online games with and he went to meet them without his parents' knowledge. He was murdered by that person on 17 February 2014. His parents have set up The Breck Foundation in his memory, which seeks to raise awareness of playing safe while using the internet.[76]

Thankfully these cases are rare, but as parents we need to be vigilant about safeguarding our children against online grooming.

WHAT PARENTS CAN DO

✓ Use parental controls and filters

Monitor and limit what your children can access on their devices (see appendix for more information).

✓ Talk about it

As with all the potential dangers for children from digital technology, it's important that we keep a sense of perspective as parents: obviously not all new contacts on social media or gaming sites are paedophiles or murderers. But we mustn't bury our heads in the sand either. In the same way as dealing with the issues of porn and sexting, it is never too early to begin a conversation with our children. Talk to younger children about grooming in the same way as you would 'stranger danger'. They should not talk privately or give personal information to anyone they don't know, whether in real life or online. Make sure they know what 'personal information' is.

---

76 The Breck Foundation, charity registration no. 1168384. http://www.breckfoundation.org.

Talk to them about the sites they use, what sorts of conversations they have and the information they share. Keeping the lines of communication open (not easy with monosyllabic teenagers) is key, so that we can make sure they are clearly aware of the dangers. In particular, we can caution them against disclosing any personal details or arranging a face-to-face meeting with someone they don't know. Our children need to know that people online aren't always who they make out they are.

Older children may well not want to be forthcoming with us about their social networks, and we'll want them to have their privacy without feeling that we are interfering. Take advantage of websites such as *www.ceop.police.uk* for advice about how to communicate with them (see appendix for more information).

We also need to remind our children they should never arrange to meet someone they only know online without an adult they trust.

✓ Watch out for changes in your child's behaviour
Unusual changes in our children's behaviour can be warning signs that they might be victims of grooming. One website, *www. internetmatters.org*, suggests that these may include the following:[77]

- Wanting to spend more and more time on the internet.
- Being secretive about who they are talking to online and what sites they visit.
- Switching screens when you come near the computer.
- Possessing items – electronic devices or phones – you haven't given them.
- Using sexual language you wouldn't expect them to know
- Becoming emotionally volatile.

Of course, secretive, emotional and 'unusual' behaviour is fairly typical of teenagers, so we shouldn't assume the worst, but if we do find our children have been the victim of grooming (our children may not even realise that's what it is) then, like Kayleigh's mother, we should contact the police.

---

77 Internetmatters.org, 'Online grooming'. https://www.internetmatters.org/issues/online-grooming.

✓ Be there for them

Let your children know that they can come to you, or another adult they trust at any time if they get into trouble online or are worried about any conversations they may be having with people.

If you think that your child is being groomed or in immediate danger report it to the police at once. You can also call the NSPCC's free adult helpline or the National Crime Agency's CEOP Command (see appendix for further information).

CHAPTER 12

INTERNET
ADDICTION

At the end of our parenting seminars, lots of people talk to us about parenting issues and top of the list of concerns are worries about too much screen time and internet addiction. Their concern is not unfounded. Shocking reports have appeared in the media of children as young as 4 being addicted to iPads and smartphones. Dr Richard Graham, who launched the UK's first technology addiction programme 3 years ago, said in an interview:

> *They see their parents playing on their mobile devices and they want to play too. It's difficult, because having a device can also be very useful in terms of having a reward, having a pacifier. But if you don't get the balance right it can be very dangerous. They can't cope and become addicted, reacting with tantrums and uncontrollable behaviour when they are taken away.*[78]

And children have gone to extraordinarily extreme lengths to ensure their online access. A 16-year-old American girl and her friend were so desperate to get around the 10 p.m. family internet curfew that they went out to the local shop, bought milkshakes for her parents, and mixed them with ground-up sleeping tablets. An hour later, the parents were slumbering peacefully leaving the girls free to use the internet as they pleased. When the parents woke in the morning with terrific hangover-like symptoms, their suspicions were aroused and they bought a cheap drug testing kit to test themselves. Before they knew it, the girls were answering questions at the local police station.[79]

An article in the *New York Post* in 2016 by Dr Nicholas Kardaras caused widespread concern among many anxious parents when

---

78 Gemma Aldridge, 'Girl aged four is Britain's youngest-known iPad addict', *The Mirror*, 21 April 2013. http://www.mirror.co.uk/news/uk-news/girl-aged-four-britains-youngest-known-1844779.
79 Amanda Holpuch, 'California teens accused of drugging parents to get around Internet curfew', *The Guardian*, 3 January 2013.

he argued that young children exposed to too much screen time were at risk of developing an addiction 'harder to kick than drugs'.[80] He reported that recent brain-imaging research confirmed that glowing screens affect the brain's prefrontal cortex in the same way as drugs like cocaine and heroin. This is the part of the brain that controls impulse and mental functions and helps us manage time, pay attention, plan, organise and remember details. He also referred to research from the US military with burn victims. While their wounds were being dressed, they normally required large doses of morphine, but when they were given a video game to play they felt no pain. While a wonderful advance in pain-management, it begs the question as to what effect this digital 'drug' is having on the brains of over-stimulated 7-year-olds who are transfixed to their glowing screens. Perhaps, then, it's no surprise that Steve Jobs was a notoriously *low-tech* parent, as are many Silicon Valley's top technology designers and engineers today.

Bradley was given his first smartphone just before he started secondary school. Before long he also had a laptop (needed for homework) and, after much pleading, an iPad. While at a friend's house he was introduced to a gaming forum and started playing video games with online friends who he never met face-to-face. He began to spend more time online, often playing until the small hours of the morning. His parents and friends noticed a change in his behaviour; he became aggressive and distant, dropped his old friends, and his mum said he stopped playing football, going to church and joining in after-school activities altogether. Bradley needed help.

Although the possibility of online activity taking over our children's lives is a real one, we need to keep a sense of perspective. Children generally don't get addicted to digital technology simply by being in contact with it, and the addictive behaviour may be due to underlying issues such as gambling, shopping or identity rather than online activity itself. Like any addiction to drugs and alcohol, the internet offers children and adolescents a way to escape

---

80 Dr Nicholas Kardaras, 'It's "digital heroin": How screens turn kids into psychotic junkies', *New York Post*, 27 August 2016.

problems, difficult situations and painful feelings. Children who don't have close friendships and who have poor social and coping skills are at greater risk of developing internet addiction. Because they feel alone, alienated, and have problems making new friends, they may turn to invisible strangers online for the attention and companionship missing in their real lives – they create a comforting online world for themselves as a means of escape.

A friend recently showed me an entertaining article by journalist Kate Roiphe, which I think helps us keep things in proportion. Here's a short extract:[81]

The other day, I did something that is, apparently, not done: I brought my seven-year-old and his friend to a playground while they were hunting for Pokémon *on an iPhone. A strong ripple of disapproval ran through assorted benched parents …*

I've been noticing that some of the parents of my son's friends refuse to let their kids play Pokémon Go *or* Minecraft, *and are mystified by or politely disapproving of my wanton permissiveness. 'We don't do that,' they say, in slightly the same tone they would use if I were letting seven-year-olds play tag in a needle-strewn crack den. In my small addict's defense, he does marshall impressive research skills in these endeavours. He has read every book on* Minecraft *in existence; at night he falls asleep studying* Pokémon *dictionaries. He is probably, I tell him, one of the world's leading experts on* Pokémon.

Meanwhile, as I write, the small addict's 13-year-old sister — I'll call her the big addict — is sprawled languorously across a couch. I ask her what she is doing but she is too languorous to do much more than whisper a barely audible response. She is, however, able to raise her arm slightly for Snapchat. While I am aware that taking a weird picture of herself, with butterflies superimposed in her hair, and sending it to a friend with an inane comment is not the highest form of human connection, I

81 Katie Roiphe 'Screen wars: parents v children', *Financial Times*, 16 December 2016.

can't say it's worse than the endless hours I used to spend on the phone with my friends, lying upside down on my bed, twirling the curly phone cord. As Danah Boyd, an internet scholar, has pointed out, hanging out is part of the work of teenage years; socialising is part of learning to be a functional adult. In It's Complicated, Boyd writes, 'Teens turn to, and are obsessed with, whichever environment allows them to connect to friends. Most teens aren't addicted to social media; if anything, they're addicted to each other.'

As parents, we'll understandably want our children not to miss out on the things that we did when we were young – making dens in the garden or tents with sheets draped over the living-room furniture, riding bikes, and playing board games – but we also don't want to prevent them from socialising and connecting with their peers. So how do we know when 'normal' activity crosses the invisible line into addictive use? How much is too much?

An addiction is a state where someone compulsively engages with a stimulus (which might be drugs, alcohol, shopping, or – as here – online activity) in a way that interferes with normal everyday life. Simon, now a father of three, admits to having a computer addiction while at university. He said:

My online activity took over my life. The more I was online the more I needed to be online to get another 'fix'. I was so immersed in my gaming that I would forget to eat and to sleep. I withdrew from flat mates and my studies began to suffer.

If we take a step back, we can see how online activity has all the raw ingredients necessary to encourage addictive behaviour, particularly with risk-taking, consequence-oblivious, impressionable teens. Addictions thrive on regular reward, generating the need for more and more, and then more again. Gaming manufacturers use this to their advantage; each stage is designed so that the player wants to go on to the next one (it certainly teaches perseverance!) Social media,

'How about you go read some parenting books
and just let me play?'

as well as gaming, also encourages compulsive behaviour by feeding an insatiable appetite for 'likes' and 'shares' fuelled by FOMO (fear of missing out). This can lead to a 24/7 checking of Instagram or Facebook pages.

But, as we said before when we looked at the effects of social media, let's not throw the baby out with the bathwater. One study found that young people who played games for an hour a day actually appeared *better* adjusted than those who didn't play games at all![82] They had fewer social or emotional problems, were happier about their friendships, were more helpful to others and were generally more satisfied with life. However, the minority who played for more than 3 hours a day seemed to be worse off. They were more likely to be hyperactive and emotionally volatile compared to those who played less or not at all. Those who played between 1 and 3 hours a day appeared no different to those who never played games. The principle we can take from this is that while we don't need to rigidly set the number of minutes our children spend gaming, as parents we ignore their excessive screen use at our peril.

Even more encouraging for those of us who are somewhat weary in monitoring our children's screen time was that the research found that only about 2% of hyperactivity and antisocial behaviour could be related to gaming. Other factors such as schooling, housing, gender and *parenting* (hurray!) had a much bigger impact on children's well-being.

WHAT PARENTS CAN DO

✓ Find out what your child is doing online
If we believe our child may have an internet addiction, it is worth finding out what it is that they are doing online. We may discover that their behaviour online is actually the result of an addiction to another activity (gambling or shopping, for example). If that is the case, we will need to seek the appropriate help for them.

82 Andrew K. Przybylski, 'Electronic gaming and psychosocial adjustment', *Pediatrics*, July 2014.

✓ Put screen time guidelines in place (see chapter 4)

Having limitations on screen time is a key strategy in combating internet addiction. Particularly at the younger end of the teenage years, it's essential to have some clear guidelines in place. Consider keeping a diary of your child's internet use with them. This will help you both learn if there are times when they use it more, or triggers that cause them to stay online a long time.

✓ Talk about it

Talk with your child about the amount of time they are spending on the internet and try to find out if there are specific reasons for this. Sometimes it can offer an escape from reality, and there may be problems that they are trying to get away from. If your child is facing problems that are causing this desire to escape, try to address those.

✓ Watch out for symptoms of possible addiction

Leading US psychiatrist Dr Jerald Block suggests that if our children are exhibiting the following four symptoms, then we might need to be concerned:[83]

1. Losing track of time while online and forgetting to eat or to sleep. The gaming, texting or social media becomes all-consuming.
2. Withdrawal – feelings of anger, tension or depression when they do not have access to the computer.
3. Tolerance – becoming increasingly resistant or tolerant to the benefits they get from the internet. Eventually they want to spend more hours online or feel they need better software or computers.
4. Negative repercussions – arguments, lies, social isolation, tiredness and low achievement.

83 NHS, 'Internet addiction', June 2008. http://www.nhs.uk/news/2008/06June/Pages/Internetaddiction.aspx.

WHEN THINGS GO WRONG

Despite our best efforts at safeguarding our children, we may find ourselves in a situation where the internet does seem to have taken over our child's life. One mum described how she believed her 15- and 12-year-old sons are both completely addicted:

> *Screen time dictates their entire lives; without it they are raging wrecks. As soon as they get out of bed, and absolutely whenever they can, and often when they shouldn't, they're gaming or on Instagram, Snapchat or Twitter. My 15-year-old is often up until 2 a.m. I go to bed, tell him his phone must be off, but he waits until I'm sleeping and then switches it back on. Our whole lives revolve around it ... It affects us all [as a family]. My husband gets angry and feels I undermine him when he tries to act. And I suppose I do, partly because switching things off causes such a lot of aggravation ... he just walks away and leaves the kids to yell at me until I give in because I am too stressed to deal with it.*

Understandable reactions for parents seeing the signs of internet addiction in their child are anger and fear. We might react by confiscating the offending digital device as a form of punishment or forcing our child to go 'cold turkey' to stop the problem. Neither of these responses are ideal, inviting our child to see us as the enemy, creating a 'them and us' atmosphere, and possibly resulting in them experiencing real withdrawal symptoms. It is much better to try and work *with* them by talking to them about the effect the amount of time they spend on screen has on both them and the family.

Tell them you love them, that you care about their happiness and that you are not blaming or condemning them but are concerned about what's happening – mention specific things you have noticed about their behaviour, such as fatigue, nervousness, giving up hobbies, etc. Next decide what the boundaries will be for limited internet use. If at all possible do this together, especially with teenagers. This will be much easier said than done (but worth it in

'I can't tell if he's seriously addicted or just a typical teen …'

the end) as the very idea of limited screen time will be very difficult for them to manage.

Before we all rush to disable the Wi-Fi and gather up our offspring's games consoles, laptops and smartphones to put in the recycling, once again, let me give a caveat: if we have teenagers in the house, we may recognise some of these symptoms as an integral part of normal teenage behaviour –unrelated to potential addiction problems. But, as their parents, we know our child best. We are in the very best position to know whether their behaviour has changed, has disrupted family life sufficiently to have crossed the line, and is a cause for concern.

If our children are showing signs of addictive behaviour, it is important to get help. If you feel that your advice is falling on deaf ears, consider involving others – such as respected family friends, youth leaders, or sports coaches – who they may listen to. And don't be afraid to seek professional help – your GP is the most obvious place to start.

CHAPTER 13

CONSUMER
CULTURE

In 1960, Professor Walter Mischel of Stanford University began the first of a series of famous studies that have come to be known as The Marshmallow Experiment. Taking a group of children aged 4–6, a researcher sat them down individually in a room free of distractions and put a marshmallow (or another treat of their choice) on a table by a chair. The researcher explained that they were going to leave the room and return in about 15 minutes. If the child waited and didn't eat the marshmallow until he came back in, they would earn a second marshmallow; if they ate it before he came back in, they would not be given a second one. A simple deal: one marshmallow now or two later. Mischel reported that some children ate their treat as soon as the researcher left the room, but others:

> *cover their eyes with their hands or turn around so that they can't see the tray, others start kicking the desk, or tug on their pigtails, or stroke the marshmallow as if it were a tiny stuffed animal.*[84]

In follow-up studies, the researchers found unexpected correlations between the results of the marshmallow test and the success of the children many years later, in all kinds of ways. Those who had been able to wait in order to receive the reward of the second treat tended to have better life outcomes as measured by educational attainment, SAT scores, body mass index and other life measures.

This simple experiment revealed what is now believed to be one of the most important factors that contribute to success in life: the power of delayed gratification.

As parents, we will want to teach our children the advantages of

---

84 Walter Mischel, et al., 'Cognitive and attentional mechanisms in delay of gratification', *Journal of Personality and Social Psychology*, 1972, vol. 21, no. 2, pp. 204–218.

'What do you mean you ate them all?! You knew
we were going to do the marshmallow test on the
kids today!'

delayed gratification – short-term pain for long-term gain! However, in this endeavour we are not taking part on a level playing field. We are competing against a culture which continually bombards them with the opposite message. One click on Amazon Prime from their smartphones 'takes the waiting out of wanting' and offers instant gratification.

Last night, I spent some time on my laptop googling vintage metal light fittings. Hoping for a hallway that rivals some of those seen on *Grand Designs*, I set out to compare and contrast what was on offer in this admittedly niche market. This morning I am being pestered and pursued by every light fitting manufacturer known to man.

Perhaps even more intriguing, returning from holiday a while ago I packed a bottle of red wine in our suitcase, cushioned (as I thought) between our swimming towels. Sadly, some energetic baggage handling at the airport resulted in the bottle exploding, with an ensuing overpowering bouquet of Rioja and a suitcase of pink clothes. Once home, I tweeted about our experience and seconds later a message came into my inbox letting me know about the Jet Bag which promised to be 'the diaper for the wine in your luggage'.

It's what is known as personal targeted advertising and it is directed just as much at brand-conscious young consumers as their adult counterparts. Social media is punctuated with sponsored advertising giving incentives to buy those must-have trainers, fake eyelashes, favourite music track, ring tone, Xbox game, or props for avatars. Teens are also increasingly using their own networks for sharing information about the latest fashion essential or once-in-a-lifetime bargain. Those of us with teenage daughters will no doubt be familiar with the phenomenon of hundreds of photos taken from assorted angles in changing rooms as different clothes are being tried on. These pictures are then sent around their friends for admiration and comment.

Of course, there is nothing new about children wanting things – new toys, gadgets, snacks, clothes, etc. – but today's parents have a harder job to combat pester power than in previous generations because of the 24/7 presence of advertising and media through digital technology. The 2011 Bailey Review 'Letting Children Be Children,'[85] an enquiry into what was described as the commercialisation and sexualisation of children, reported that:

> Nearly nine out of 10 parents surveyed for this Review agreed with the statement that 'these days children are under pressure to grow up too quickly' ... This pressure on children to grow up takes two different but related forms: the pressure to take part in a sexualised life before they are ready to do so; and the commercial pressure to consume the vast range of goods and services that are available to children and young people of all ages.

However, the recognised impact of online media on young people is possibly less about advertising and the pressure to buy, buy, buy and more about 'brand and lifestyle'. Many older children are increasingly savvy and recognise the power of commercial sales and marketing, but the subtle pressure of a makeup demonstration on YouTube or an Instagram fashionista modelling the latest trends may be more difficult to recognise and resist.

Online games can offer instant upgrades while your children are playing them – so if the account is set up in your name and the bill is paid by you, that summer holiday to Spain might be in jeopardy. My brother found to his cost that it just takes a moment to run up a crazy bill:

> Our 13-year-old used his first phone for messaging his friends and playing games. There were a couple of apps on it that not only allowed him to play games but invited him to click 'yes' to various premium lines. At the end of the month I was horrified to receive a bill for £340. A call to Watchdog made the phone company spring into action and refund the money, but the result could have been so different.

85 Reg Bailey, 'Letting Children Be Children. Report of an Independent Review of the Commercialisation and Sexualisation of Childhood', Department of Education, 2011.

'Good afternoon, madam. You were just googling
"How to remove carpet stains". Can I show you the
SuckCleaner 2000? It's a complete cleaning system for
all your cleaning needs ...'

In-app purchases can also catch us unawares. Games that are 'free-to-play' may be free to download and play on a basic level, but the catch is that you have to spend money to improve the game experience – to move up a level, for example. Often it is the only way to compete if you are playing against another person who has spent money on the game. Some in-app purchases can even be renewable, like monthly subscriptions that repeat until you cancel them.

Another issue is the ease with which young people online can pull the wool over the eyes of suppliers about their age. While it may be difficult for most fresh-faced 15-year-olds to buy that bottle of vodka at the local off-licence even with fake ID, underage purchases are made with apparent ease online. I remember setting up a family investigation to rival the Chilcot Inquiry after an over-18 game mysteriously arrived in the post; the only people in the house over 18 were my husband and myself, and we certainly hadn't placed the order.

But while it can be stressful and expensive for their parents, how harmful is a child's increased exposure to consumer pressures? A British study found that consumerism is not a benign influence on our children and that it can result in them being depressed and anxious.[86] Further evidence also suggests that children who place a high value on what they own have a greater tendency for depression as well as loneliness, insecurity, general discontentment and social problems.[87] They are more likely to believe that possessions bring happiness, that success is defined by what they own, and that the primary goal in life is to acquire material goods and the admiration of others.

WHAT PARENTS CAN DO

✓ Remember that young children are particularly vulnerable to advertising
Research suggests that until the ages of about 7 or 8, children do not understand the true purpose of advertisements – seeing it as another

86 P. Graham, 'The good childhood – a national inquiry: evidence summary four – lifestyle', The Children's Society, 2008.
87 D. Bee-Gates, 'Consumer Culture: Confronting materialism while raising children', Parentguide News. http://www.parentguidenews.com/Catalog/ConsumerCulture.

form of entertainment or information-sharing.[88] One researcher pointed out that, 'Younger children aren't even able to understand that ads, which are now cropping up in video games and movies, online and even in cell phones, are intended to sell them things.'[89] Unsurprisingly, perhaps, the researchers discovered that the more time California third-graders spent watching TV or playing video games, the more often they asked an adult to buy them the items they saw on the screen.

✓ Limit their exposure
Use parental controls to actively monitor your children's online screen time (see chapter 4).

✓ Talk about spending
It's never too early to talk to our children about money and the relentless pressure to buy, and learning to shop both offline and online teaches important lessons for life. We can give pocket money for sweets or comics when they are little, teaching them to budget and allowing them more responsibility with money as they get older. We can have family discussions about the pitfalls of online shopping – hidden delivery costs, fake websites, the possibility of stolen bank account details – and we can let them know that if a bargain seems like it's too good to be true, it probably is! Remember that the more informed a child is about money, the less likely they are to spend it unthinkingly or as a means of comfort when under emotional pressure.

✓ Give them your time
After its report in 2007 showed that child well-being in the UK was at the bottom of a list of developed nations, Unicef concluded four years later that the reason was because we assign too little importance to family time, and too much to material goods.[90] It

---

88 Karen J. Pine, et al, 'The Relationship Between Television Advertising, Children's Viewing and Their Requests to Father Christmas', *Journal of Developmental & Behavioral Pediatrics*, 2007, vol. 28, no. 6, pp. 456-461.
89 'Watch not, want not? Kids' TV time tied to consumerism', *Standford News*, 12 April 2006. http://news.stanford.edu/news/2006/april12/med-tv-041206.html.
90 Mark Easton, 'Our children need time not stuff', *BBC News*, 13 September 2011. http://www.bbc.co.uk/news/uk-14899148.

argued that the pressure of the working environment and endemic materialism damaged the well-being of children:

> *All children interviewed said that material goods did not make them happy, but materialism in the UK seems to be just as much of a problem for parents as for children ... they work all hours to increase family income, but then are too exhausted or too busy to give their children the attention they need and deserve.*

Comparing Britain with Sweden and Spain (who came second and fifth respectively in the child well-being table), the researchers found that in both countries 'family time is protected' and children 'all have greater access to activities'.[91] Of course, people in these countries were also materialistic, but they seemed to find it easier to refuse to buy goods for their children and family life, and time for the extended family was more protected:

> *In terms of children's well-being, the study found that time spent with family was what really brought satisfaction. 'It came out loud and clear that children want to spend time with their family and friends.'*

Although the well-being of British children has improved in a number of areas in recent years, it continues to lag behind that of many of their European neighbours.

✓ Help your children become media-savvy

Over the age of around 7 or 8, children are able to understand about advertising tactics, so start talking to them about this early on. Explain that adverts are created by companies to make people believe their products are going to make us feel better, have more fun, be prettier, be stronger, or make life better in some other way. They also make people think they need or want something that they never knew about and now feel they must have – right now!

91 *Ibid.*

Some of our friends used to play what they called 'the advert game' with their children. During the commercial breaks on the TV they would have a competition to be the first to spot the 'lie' in the promotion.

You can help your children become more media-savvy by looking together at an online advertisement that they know well and asking them what it is doing to make the product seem like something they need. Does the advert make it look bigger than in real life (often the case with toy adverts)? Do the people look happy (suggesting that you would be happy if you had the product)? Does the advert feature famous actors, singers or sports personalities to make you think the product is good? Does it promote the product by giving you something for free with it, or scare you by saying that you need to hurry to buy it before the 'sale ends'?

With older children, help them think about how the advert was targeted at them. Is it based on the content of other sites they have visited (contextually targeted)? Or is it targeted at them because of online information about them – searches they have made, online purchases, browsing history (behaviourally targeted)? Ask them to search a term on their own device, and then to search the same term on your device and see if the results are different. Children can be really surprised when they realise how their personal information and actions determine what adverts they see.

Also, with older children, talk about the way adverts sell ideas as well as products – for example, how they link products with the 'perfect' life portrayed by the people in the adverts, or with a happy family life, or a romantic relationship … [ask them to fill in the blanks].

'They play so well together ...'

CHAPTER 14

ALL KINDS OF FAMILIES – ALL KINDS OF ISSUES!

Families come in all shapes and sizes, and digital technology will bring different benefits and concerns in different parenting situations. In this chapter, we're going to look at some common family situations.

Carol and Ben are the parents of 13-year-old Tom.

Scene 1. In the car: From the moment she picks Tom up from school, Carol knows that it's going to be a long evening. Ignoring the grumpy face and brooding silence in the back, she asks brightly how his day has been. Experience has given her low expectations as to his response. He doesn't disappoint!

Scene 2. At home: The evening goes as anticipated: rows over hanging up his coat, homework, turning off the TV and sitting down at the table for tea. An innocent remark from his sister results in Tom kicking her on the shins and sending her flying backwards. Carol finally snaps. She dispatches Tom to his bedroom and tells him his games console is confiscated until the next day, and, in any event, until he apologises to his sister.

Scene 3. Enter Ben: Ben has had a good day at work and is looking forwarding to catching up with the children before they go to bed. Carol tells him what has happened, and he goes upstairs to chat to Tom.

Scene 4. 10 minutes later: Carol hears shouts of delight from the living room and pokes her head around the door only to see father and son engaged in a game of *FIFA* on the confiscated games console.

Scene 5. 11 minutes later: Probably best left to the imagination!

If we are parenting together, it is vital that as far as possible we remain united on matters of discipline and boundaries. There have been many occasions when, in the heat of the moment, either Richard or I have meted out an all too draconian punishment – no Xbox until the end of the year (but it's only 1st January), no birthday party (but half the class have already been invited), no trip to the cinema (but it's with Granny and we have already bought the tickets) … At such times, it takes all the willpower in the universe not to undermine the other parent by immediately stepping in and siding with the child. If we (or our partner) have acted hastily and imposed unilateral sanctions worthy of foreign office diplomacy, we need to try to step back, apologise where necessary and accept that there is scope for undoing them. We all make mistakes and act in the heat of the moment, and as long as it's not a daily occurrence, these moments give a great opportunity to model apology and forgiveness in the family. Being united on discipline and boundaries is just as important when it comes to digital use. If there is a chink of light between you, most savvy 10-year-olds will be right in there and able to use it to their advantage. Giving a clear, consistent, and united message as a couple brings security to family life.

For single parents, the task of monitoring our children's digital use can be particularly challenging. It's hard enough with two pairs of eyes and two pairs of hands, so with half that resource the task can be immense.

Most of us, but especially those parenting on their own, will at some point have needed to sit our toddler in front of a screen simply in order to have a shower or take a work call. A single parent dad commented:

> *Single parents often let their children stay online for longer so they can have some down time or just get the things done. They may be exhausted and if their children ask for 15 minutes and then 15 minutes more they may say yes just to have peace and quiet. I've learnt not to go on a guilt trip, but once in a while*

try finding something non-digital to keep them quiet while you just catch up on jobs.

Looking back to when her son was younger, another single parent talked about the benefits that digital technology has given them both:

I remember when we bought my son his first mobile. He was still in junior school, and I thought at the time that he was too young to own a phone. However, all his friends had one, and as a parent, you want your children to be able to be kept up to date with technology as the world progresses. Maybe I was being too old-fashioned, I thought. Fast forward a year from this date, and I am now a single parent. For me in this situation, my son owning a mobile phone is something that I rely on to communicate with him. I can contact him when he is at his dad's, when I'm at work – anytime, and my son can contact me.

As a single parent, you can't be everywhere all the time, and technology has helped me to be able to stay in contact in a way that I wouldn't have been able to in the past, before mobile phones. Using technology has helped me to have more peace of mind as I can communicate with my children, know they are OK, and know they can contact me at any time.

Kat told me that she wasn't very tech-savvy when she became a single parent. She could use a computer, but as far as firewalls and security goes, she really didn't have a clue. Desperately wanting to protect her family online but not knowing how to go about doing it, she attended an evening her daughter's school was running for parents on internet safety.

The teachers spoke to us about how to place parental controls on our computers and told us about a program that we could get to keep an eye on what the children were accessing online and who they were speaking to. I contacted a friend who was a computer technician and asked him to install the program onto my children's laptop. This program came in very handy and I would strongly encourage any parent to go to any event like the one I went to, especially single parents as we don't have someone at home that can help us with these things.

Many of the challenges single parents face are not because they are parenting alone: they are issues common to *every* parent. But life can be tough as a single mum or dad. Having less time and ability to supervise children's online activity, as well as setting and defending the boundaries alone isn't easy. If you are parenting alone don't be afraid to ask for and accept help. If keeping up with digital technology is really not your thing, ask a trusted friend or colleague to help you set up parental controls.

Many single parents or blended families may be trying to keep an eye on digital use across two households. Having consistent guidelines and safeguards is particularly helpful – and lots of parents in this situation are able to put this in place effectively. Sometimes, however, these arrangements don't run smoothly. Jon's children spend half the week with him and the other half with their mum and her partner. Jon reflects:

We divorced when the kids were quite young, so they are used to dividing their week between both homes, but it has got more difficult as they have got older. Their mum's partner has older children from a previous relationship, and I find they are playing 15+ games there, which our kids are not old enough to do. It's hard as they are spending half the week in a place with different values and where you have no control.

Lisa had a similar experience:

My ex was the typical permissive parent. He gave the children no boundaries at all, and he encouraged them to watch movies or play games that they weren't allowed to watch in

'Hi, Dad. Yes, I'm still at nursery, but there's a problem!
Sarah won't share the toys again. Can you come and
sort it out?'

my home because they were not appropriate for their age. I tried to discuss creating some digital rules that we could agree so that the children had boundaries across both homes and wouldn't get confused. I would always stress that this was for our children's well-being and the focus was on them, not us. Unfortunately, the majority of the time, my ex was never too interested in laying down boundaries. He wanted to be the children's 'friend' and parented in this manner.

In view of this, I had to decide what to do in my home. Should I allow my children to play video games and watch movies that were inappropriate for their age? Should I let them go online as much as they liked? I eventually decided that I would continue to keep the boundaries that I felt were right for the well-being, safety and protection of my children. I often wondered if I was doing the right thing and whether I was being too strict. My friends were a great support to me, encouraged me to hold the line, and said that even if my ex had a different approach these boundaries would help my children in the long run. I didn't always get it right, but overall, while I could not control what happened at their dad's house, I could control what happened in mine.

If you are co-parenting, if at all possible try to agree some guidelines for digital use that can be consistently applied in both homes. This will be easier to do in some situations than in others, especially if you initially have differing views, but if you can come to an agreement it will be a win-win, for the children and for you both. But be prepared. Some co-parenting situations are very challenging, so that kind of negotiation may not always be possible. It certainly isn't for the faint-hearted and may involve some give and take on both sides.

Foster parents can face a particular challenge when it comes to setting boundaries on technology use. Jon Trew, a foster parent himself and trainer in child protection and safety online, describes the problem in Vodafone magazine:[92]

92 *Digital Parenting* magazine, Issue 4, https://www.vodafone.com/content/dam/vodafone-images/parents/assets-2016/pdf/Digital_ParentingMagazine_Issue_4.pdf.

Newly fostered children often arrive with mobile devices they've brought from their previous home. They may have been allowed to view unsuitable material or to stay up late online … It can be a challenge to change such habits, but it's not impossible. It's best to establish ground rules regarding online time immediately, just as you would with any other house rules. It's also important to be realistic: telling a child that they can use the computer only where you can see them isn't going to work in a mobile age!

It is estimated that there are currently fourteen million grandparents in the UK who provide childcare for their grandchildren, and many more are in close regular contact with them. A grandparent can be the voice of reassurance and reason speaking wisdom into children's lives over the years. Whether it's the 6-year-old who wants a sexy bra and high heels to look like her favourite singer on the latest music video, the 10-year-old who has stumbled across porn, or the image-conscious but slightly overweight 14-year-old who has been defriended by her best friend on Facebook, grandparents can give their grandchildren the most precious of gifts: the reassurance that they are loved simply for who they are.

Whether grandparents engage with their grandchildren face-to-face or across the miles, use of digital devices will almost certainly play a part. A newspaper article this week had the title, 'Dear Granny, thanks for my present. Love from me and my new app.'[93] Digital card manufacturers have created software that can not only print a personal picture on a card, but replicate the child's handwriting and have it delivered on their behalf. Gone are the days of enforced writing of thank-you letters to grandparents on Boxing Day (or in our case, 15th January!). A friend who is a wonderful granny had a birthday card created by her 8-year-old granddaughter on an iPad. While, admittedly, it couldn't join the array of cards on the mantelpiece, she loved the time and effort that had gone into creating it. My mother is a great texter, and if grandchildren come

93 Fariha Karim, 'Dear Granny, thanks for my present. Love from me and my new app', *The Times*, 6 January 2017.

along will be a text-savvy great-grandmother. She has a phone with a big enough screen to see easily, and she tells me she prefers texting to phoning as she doesn't worry she is interrupting, but most of all it gives her a great means of connection with the wider family, especially the grandchildren. Next week I am meeting her for coffee to teach her the delights of WhatsApp.

If grandparents are doing hands-on childcare, however informal the arrangement, the generation gap can mean that there is a difference of opinion about digital use, so communication about the boundaries is key. Each family is different, but if the friction isn't easily resolved, giving grandparents the freedom (within limits) to agree digital guidelines when they are in charge, or at the very least when the children are in their home, might be a good place to start.

Modern technology makes grandparenting at a distance easier than ever, and those who are separated geographically from their grandchildren sometimes have as much interaction with them as those who live nearby. In *The Sixty Minute Grandparent*,[94] Rob Parsons tells the story of a grandfather who had described himself as a technophobe but became a regular Skype user because, as he put it, 'I realised if I wanted to be part of my grandchildren's everyday lives then I had better pull my finger out and get with it.' It's not true for everyone of course, but more and more grandparents are using Skype, social media and online games to connect with their grandchildren. One granny we know has written a lovely story with her grandson. She would write a paragraph and email it to him, and then he would write the next bit and so on. It was not only a fun activity for him, but built what is now a very special relationship between them.

---

94 Rob Parsons, *The Sixty Minute Grandparent*, Hodder, 2013, p. 84.

CHAPTER 15

TEACHING THEM TO
LEARN TO DISCERN

A family walk recently took us along a beautiful Pembrokeshire coastal path. It was a January day and the sky was bright blue with not a cloud in sight. We paused on the clifftop to enjoy the view. Stretching to the horizon in one direction was a patchwork of green fields, and in the other we could see the reassuring rhythm of the waves as they glistened in the winter sun. We breathed in the sea air ... it was good to be alive.

After a few moments, we clambered down onto the beach and walked across the sand, making our way around the edge of a cliff. And then we saw it ... a red flag fluttering in the breeze high up on the dunes. Our path had inadvertently taken us onto the MOD firing range. In a moment, the afternoon no longer felt so relaxed and carefree. We needed to pay attention and choose our route home rather more carefully.

I later reflected that this path, which offers its walkers such breathtaking scenery and new horizons, at the very same time has the potential to kill, harm and destroy unless it is followed very carefully. As parents, how do we teach our children to walk the path of digital engagement wisely, making the most of the incredible opportunities it offers while equipping them to steer clear of the dangers?

As we've discussed, there are age-appropriate external safeguards that we can put in place to protect our children which are absolutely vital, particularly when they are young: passwords, filters, parental controls, family internet agreements. But those external controls simply aren't enough.

It was the first term at secondary school and one of our boys asked if he could go to a friend's birthday sleepover. We didn't know the parents well, but all his friends were going and we said yes. It was some time later that we found out that much of the time there had been spent looking at pornographic images on the dad's computer.

We can put every protection in the universe in place, our home can be a digitally impenetrable Fort Knox with every safeguard known to man installed, but it doesn't protect our children when they are away from home. In the playground, at a neighbour's house, in the changing rooms after a match, with a friend whose parents have different values to our own or who don't implement external safeguards themselves – there's the potential for them to download anything on the planet.

It is easy to feel overwhelmed by the dangers – real and imagined – that they may face living in a digital culture, but as we've already seen, as their parents we really are the biggest influence in our children's lives – bigger than any social media platform, *Minecraft*, *Pokémon*, *FIFA*, *Battlefield* or any other game of the moment. There's so much to play for!

It's often said that values are more often caught than taught. Sometimes we think our children aren't listening to us; in fact, the problem is quite the opposite. While filming Care for the Family's DVD course *Parentalk in the Primary Years*, we interviewed Jon, a dad with two boys aged 10 and 8. He had a demanding job and took full advantage of the 24/7 access to his emails that his smartphone gave him to help him keep his inbox under control. One of his boys saw his father's phone in a different light. One Saturday morning as Jon was replying to some emails, he heard his son asking him a question but wasn't really listening and didn't reply. His son persisted, 'Daddy, can we go to the park? … Daddy …' Irritated, Jon looked up and said, 'Can't you see I'm busy?' In sheer frustration, his son replied, 'Dad you're much nicer without your iPhone.' Ouch! For that young father, it was a wake-up call.

Journalist Katie Roiphe made a similar point when she wrote about her 7-year-old's observations:[95]

> *[He] often points out that in the exact moment I am telling him to get off his iPad, I am glancing at my email. He is rightfully outraged that my stupid addiction is somehow*

95 Katie Roiphe, 'Screen wars: parents v children', *Financial Times*, 16 December 2016.

perfectly acceptable and even laudable adult behaviour, while his is rotting his brain. His addiction is somehow stunting him, dashing his attention span and perverting his ability to live in the moment but mine is just, you know, keeping up with the office and following political news in a responsible way.

And we are role models to our children not just in how we use digital media but in every aspect of our lives. They notice the value that we place on relationships, on money, on the environment, on our health, on our possessions, on issues of faith, on how we treat others, particularly those who have less than we do. They don't miss a thing.

While there are no guarantees, little by little through the conversations, the time spent together and the everyday ups and the downs of family life, intentionally and unintentionally over the years we will be sowing values into our children's lives that will become the reference point for their own decision-making in the years to come.

Our role as parents is a positive one. We don't just have to leave our children to their own devices either in the digital world or the wider world. Instead of being naysayers, we can teach our children to manage their freedom well, training them from the inside out to make wise choices in a world where all choices are possible. We do this by placing values in their hearts that will be the compass for their lives. When we live out our values in the context of our family life, we'll be building into our children's lives the confidence and wisdom not to just go with the flow, but empowering them to make *good* choices. To learn to discern.

The writer in the ancient book of Proverbs said this about wisdom:

> *Do not forsake wisdom, and she will protect you;*
> *love her, and she will watch over you.*
> *Wisdom is supreme; therefore get wisdom.*[96]

That, I imagine, is what we want for all of our children.

96 Proverbs 4:6–7, NIV.

'Time to turn that thing off now, Dad.
I think you're getting addicted to it ...'

EPILOGUE

The rain is hammering against Alice's bedroom window as she throws her school bag onto her bed. She can hear her little brothers squabbling downstairs. It's 7.15 p.m. and already dark, so she draws the curtains. She has a school science project to complete and turns on her laptop. Before getting going, she notices that Karl is online. He is 15. Karl speaks first:

```
Hi Alice. I've seen you on the bus. You're
in the year below me, aren't you?
Yes.
You're very pretty.
Thank you.
Alice, undo the top three buttons on your
shirt. [Long pause]
```

Alice's hand reaches for her top button. As she does, her mind goes back to a hundred conversations with her mum and her dad – over dinner, in the car, late at night sitting at the end of their bed. She remembers the chat they had during that TV programme, the laughter and the tears in the ups and downs of family life, the talk she had that summer with her grandad, and the discussions she and her friends had with their youth leader. And suddenly she knows …. deep, deep down in her inmost being … she has to prove herself to nobody.

In that moment, her hand moves away from the button on her shirt and Alice hears herself say …

```
No.
```

As parents we are teaching our children to 'learn to discern' not only in the area of digital engagement but also with regard to all the big issues of life.

We're playing for that 'No'.

APPENDIX

Further help and support

The following organisations have published helpful advice and guidance on the issues described in this book. Much of this information is for parents, but there are also some helpline contact details for anyone to use. Specific web addresses obviously change from time to time, so you may need to find the article you are looking for by searching from an organisation's home page or a general web browser.

ⓘ BBC WebWise
www.bbc.co.uk/webwise
A guide to the internet with articles on a variety of subjects including parental tools.

ⓘ Bullying UK
www.bullying.co.uk
Helpline: 0808 800 2222
Information and advice on bullying specifically, as well as other challenges facing children in the digital world. There is a help line (free even on mobiles) and live chat.

ⓘ CEOP (Child Exploitation & Online Protection Centre)
www.ceop.police.uk
Internet safety advice for parents and carers with a 'virtual police station' to report abuse on the internet.

ⓘ Care for the Family
www.careforthefamily.org.uk
A national charity that aims to promote strong family life and help those who face family difficulties. It provides parenting, relationship and bereavement support through events, resources, courses, training and volunteer networks.

ⓘ Childline
www.childline.org.uk
Helpline: 0800 1111
A free 24-hour counselling service for children and young people up to their 19th birthday in the UK, provided by the NSPCC. Childline deals with any issue that causes distress or concern, including online bullying, safety and abuse online.

ⓘ Childnet International
www.childnet.com
Information for children about the latest websites and services they like to use: mobiles, gaming, downloading, social networking and more. A section for parents includes helpful information about what children and young people are doing online, together with useful ways to keep your child safe.

ⓘ Common Sense Media
www.commonsensemedia.org
Information, advice, and innovative tools to help harness the power of media and technology as a positive force in all children's lives.

ⓘ Get Safe Online
www.getsafeonline.org
Practical advice on how to protect yourself, your computers and mobile devices, and your business against fraud, identity theft, viruses and other problems encountered online. Includes a specific section on safeguarding children.

ⓘ Internet Matters
www.internetmatters.org
Information and advice to help parents keep their children safe online, covering issues such as online bullying, online grooming, inappropriate content, pornography, self-harm.

❶ NSPCC

www.nspcc.org.uk
Helpline: 0800 800 5000
A national charity helping children who have been abused to rebuild their lives, protecting those at risk, and finding the best ways of preventing abuse from ever happening. Website includes information and advice about online safety issues.

❶ Parent Zone

www.parentzone.org.uk
General advice on family life with sections on the digital world.

❶ Place2Be

www.place2be.org.uk
A children's mental health charity providing in-school support and expert training to improve the emotional well-being of pupils, families, teachers and school staff.

❶ Romance Academy

www.romanceacademy.org
Resources, events and training to help you talk effectively with your children about relationships and sex.

❶ Safer Internet Centre

www.saferinternet.org.uk
Advice and support on online safety issues, including an anonymous hotline to report and remove child sexual abuse imagery and videos wherever they are found in the world. There is also a helpline for professionals working with children and young people with online safety issues.

❶ Young Minds

www.youngminds.org.uk
Helpline for parents: 0800 802 5544
Help and support for children, parents and professionals concerning mental health issues.

❶ The Naked Truth Project
www.thenakedtruthproject.com
Practical support, resources and workshops to tackle the damaging impact of pornography, including an online guide for parents.

❶ Thinkuknow
www.thinkuknow.co.uk
A range of helpful information for children, young people, parents, carers and professionals, including games and advice for specific age groups.

❶ Vodafone Digital Parenting
www.vodafone.com/content/digital-parenting.html
Advice, support, and practical 'how to' guides for keeping your children safe online.

SPECIFIC INFORMATION

❶ Checking your child's web history
home.bt.com/tech-gadgets/internet/how-to-check-your-childs-web-browser-history-11363878002352.

❶ Family internet agreements
www.childnet.com/blog/family-agreement
http://family.disney.co.uk/uk-internet-agreement
www.wisekids.org.uk/wisekidsacceptableuse.pdf

❶ Parental controls and filters
www.bbc.co.uk/webwise/0/21259412
www.internetmatters.org/parental-controls/interactive-guide
www.childnet.com/parents-and-carers/hot-topics/parental-controls
www.nspcc.org.uk/preventing-abuse/keeping-children-safe/online-safety/parental-controls

❶ Removing abusive posts
www.thinkuknow.co.uk/14_plus/help/Contact-social-sites
www.bullying.co.uk/cyberbullying/what-to-do-if-you-re-being-bullied-on-a-social-network

❶ Guides to children's apps, games and sites
www.commonsensemedia.org
www.net-aware.org.uk

❶ Social media
www.gov.uk/government/publications/child-safety-online-a-practical-guide-for-parents-and-carers/child-safety-online-a-practical-guide-for-parents-and-carers-whose-children-are-using-social-media

❶ Talking to children about online safety, privacy sexting, porn and grooming
NSPCC – Keeping Children Safe section
- Sexting: *www.nspcc.org.uk/preventing-abuse/keeping-children-safe/sexting*
- Online porn: *www.nspcc.org.uk/preventing-abuse/keeping-children-safe/online-porn*
- Talking about difficult topics: *www.nspcc.org.uk/preventing-abuse/keeping-children-safe/talking-about-difficult-topics*
- Underwear rule: *www.nspcc.org.uk/preventing-abuse/keeping-children-safe/underwear-rule*

www.thinkuknow.co.uk/14_plus/Films/Exposed
www.childline.org.uk/info-advice/bullying-abuse-safety/online-mobile-safety/sexting/zipit-app